Investigative Report on the U.S. National Security Issues Posed by Chinese Telecommunications Companies Huawei and ZTE

A report by Chairman Mike Rogers and Ranking Member C.A. Dutch Ruppersberger of the Permanent Select Committee on Intelligence

U.S. House of Representatives

112th Congress

October 8, 2012

Contents

House Permanent Select Committee on Intelligence

Chairman and Ranking Member Investigative Report on

The U.S. National Security Issues Posed by Chinese Telecommunications Companies Huawei and ZTE

Executive Summary

In February 2011, Huawei Technologies Company, the leading Chinese telecommunications equipment manufacturer, published an open letter to the U.S. Government denying security concerns with the company or its equipment, and requesting a full investigation into its corporate operations.[1] Huawei apparently believed – correctly – that without a full investigation into its corporate activities, the United States could not trust its equipment and services in U.S. telecommunications networks.[2]

The House Permanent Select Committee on Intelligence (herein referred to as "the Committee") initiated this investigation in November 2011 to inquire into the counterintelligence and security threat posed by Chinese telecommunications companies doing business in the United States. Prior to initiating the formal investigation, the Committee performed a preliminary review of the issue, which confirmed significant gaps in available information about the Chinese telecommunications sector, the histories and operations of specific companies operating in the United States, and those companies' potential ties to the Chinese state. Most importantly, that preliminary review highlighted the potential security threat posed by Chinese telecommunications companies with potential ties to the Chinese government or military. In particular, to the extent these companies are influenced by the state, or provide Chinese intelligence services access to telecommunication networks, the opportunity exists for further economic and foreign espionage by a foreign nation-state already known to be a major perpetrator of cyber espionage.

As many other countries show through their actions, the Committee believes the telecommunications sector plays a critical role in the safety and security of our nation, and is thus a target of foreign intelligence services. The

Committee's formal investigation focused on Huawei and ZTE, the top two Chinese telecommunications equipment manufacturers, as they seek to market their equipment to U.S. telecommunications infrastructure. The Committee's main goal was to better understand the level of risk posed to the United States as these companies hope to expand in the United States. To evaluate the threat, the investigation involved two distinct yet connected parts: (1) a review of open-source information on the companies' histories, operations, financial information, and potential ties to the Chinese government or Chinese Communist Party; and (2) a review of classified information, including a review of programs and efforts of the U.S. Intelligence Community (IC) to ascertain whether the IC is appropriately prioritizing and resourced for supply chain risk evaluation.[3]

Despite hours of interviews, extensive and repeated document requests, a review of open-source information, and an open hearing with witnesses from both companies, the Committee remains unsatisfied with the level of cooperation and candor provided by each company. Neither company was willing to provide sufficient evidence to ameliorate the Committee's concerns. Neither company was forthcoming with detailed information about its formal relationships or regulatory interaction with Chinese authorities. Neither company provided specific details about the precise role of each company's Chinese Communist Party Committee. Furthermore, neither company provided detailed information about its operations in the United States. Huawei, in particular, failed to provide thorough information about its corporate structure, history, ownership, operations, financial arrangements, or management. Most importantly, neither company provided sufficient internal documentation or other evidence to support the limited answers they did provide to Committee investigators.

During the investigation, the Committee received information from industry experts and current and former Huawei employees suggesting that Huawei, in particular, may be violating United States laws. These allegations describe a company that has not followed United States legal obligations or international standards of business behavior. The Committee will be referring these allegations to Executive Branch agencies for further review, including possible investigation.

In sum, the Committee finds that the companies failed to provide evidence that would satisfy any fair and full investigation. Although this alone does not prove wrongdoing, it factors into the Committee's conclusions below. Further, this report contains a classified annex, which also adds to the Committee's concerns about the risk to the United States. The investigation concludes that the risks associated with Huawei's and ZTE's provision of equipment to U.S. critical infrastructure could undermine core U.S. national-security interests.

Based on this investigation, the Committee provides the following recommendations:

Recommendation 1: The United States should view with suspicion the continued penetration of the U.S. telecommunications market by Chinese telecommunications companies.

- The United States Intelligence Community (IC) must remain vigilant and focused on this threat. The IC should actively seek to keep cleared private sector actors as informed of the threat as possible.

- The Committee on Foreign Investment in the United States (CFIUS) must block acquisitions, takeovers, or mergers involving Huawei and ZTE given the threat to U.S. national security interests. Legislative proposals seeking to expand CFIUS to include purchasing agreements should receive thorough consideration by relevant Congressional committees.

- U.S. government systems, particularly sensitive systems, should not include Huawei or ZTE equipment, including component parts. Similarly, government contractors – particularly those working on contracts for sensitive U.S. programs – should exclude ZTE or Huawei equipment in their systems.

Recommendation 2: Private-sector entities in the United States are strongly encouraged to consider the long-term security risks associated with doing business with either ZTE or Huawei for equipment or services. U.S. network providers and systems developers are strongly encouraged to seek other vendors for their projects. Based on available classified and unclassified information, Huawei and

ZTE cannot be trusted to be free of foreign state influence and thus pose a security threat to the United States and to our systems.

Recommendation 3: Committees of jurisdiction within the U.S. Congress and enforcement agencies within the Executive Branch should investigate the unfair trade practices of the Chinese telecommunications sector, paying particular attention to China's continued financial support for key companies.

Recommendation 4: Chinese companies should quickly become more open and transparent, including listing on a western stock exchange with advanced transparency requirements, offering more consistent review by independent third-party evaluators of their financial information and cyber-security processes, complying with U.S. legal standards of information and evidentiary production, and obeying all intellectual-property laws and standards. Huawei, in particular, must become more transparent and responsive to U.S. legal obligations.

Recommendation 5: Committees of jurisdiction in the U.S. Congress should consider potential legislation to better address the risk posed by telecommunications companies with nation-state ties or otherwise not clearly trusted to build critical infrastructure. Such legislation could include increasing information sharing among private sector entities, and an expanded role for the CFIUS process to include purchasing agreements.

Report

I.   **The threat posed to U.S. national-security interests by vulnerabilities in the telecommunications supply chain is an increasing priority given: the country's reliance on interdependent critical infrastructure systems; the range of threats these systems face; the rise in cyber espionage; and the growing dependence all consumers have on a small group of equipment providers.**

The United States' critical infrastructure, and in particular its telecommunications networks, depend on trust and reliability. Telecommunications networks are vulnerable to malicious and evolving intrusions or disruptive activities. A sufficient level of trust, therefore, with both the provider of the equipment and those performing managed services must exist at all times. A company providing such equipment, and particularly any company having access to or detailed knowledge of the infrastructures' architectural blueprints, must be trusted to comply with United States laws, policies, and standards. If it cannot be trusted, then the United States and others should question whether the company should operate within the networks of our critical infrastructure.

The risk posed to U.S. national-security and economic interests by cyber-threats is an undeniable priority. First, the country's reliance on telecommunications infrastructure includes more than consumers' use of computer systems. Rather, multiple critical infrastructure systems depend on information transmission through telecommunications systems. These modern critical infrastructures include electric power grids; banking and finance systems; natural gas, oil, and water systems; and rail and shipping channels; each of which depend on computerized control systems. Further, system interdependencies among these critical infrastructures greatly increase the risk that failure in one system will cause failures or disruptions in multiple critical infrastructure systems.[4] Therefore, a disruption in telecommunication networks can have devastating effects on all aspects of modern American living, causing shortages and stoppages that ripple throughout society.

Second, the security vulnerabilities that come along with this dependence are quite broad, and range from insider threats[5] to cyber espionage and attacks from sophisticated nation states. In fact, there is a growing recognition of vulnerabilities resulting from foreign-sourced telecommunications supply chains used for U.S. national-security applications. The FBI, for example, has assessed with high confidence that threats to the supply chain from both nation-states and criminal elements constitute a high cyber threat.[6] Similarly, the National Counterintelligence Executive assessed that "foreign attempts to collect U.S. technological and economic information will continue at a high level and will represent a growing and persistent threat to US economic security."[7]

Third, the U.S. government must pay particular attention to products produced by companies with ties to regimes that present the highest and most advanced espionage threats to the U.S., such as China. Recent cyber-attacks often emanate from China, and even though precise attribution is a perennial challenge, the volume, scale, and sophistication often indicate state involvement. As the U.S.-China Commission explained in its unclassified report on China's capabilities to conduct cyber warfare and computer network exploitation (CNE), actors in China seeking sensitive economic and national security information through malicious cyber operations often face little chance of being detected by their targets.[8]

Finally, complicating this problem is the fact that Chinese telecommunications firms, such as Huawei and ZTE, are rapidly becoming dominant global players in the telecommunications market. In another industry, this development might not be particularly concerning. When those companies seek to control the market for sensitive equipment and infrastructure that could be used for spying and other malicious purposes, the lack of market diversity becomes a national concern for the United States and other countries.[9] Of note, the United States is not the only country focusing on these concerns. Australia expressed similar concerns when it chose to ban Huawei from its national broadband infrastructure project.[10] Great Britain has attempted to address the concerns by instituting an evaluation regime that limits Huawei's access to the infrastructure and evaluates any Huawei equipment and software before they enter the infrastructure.[11]

A. China has the means, opportunity, and motive to use telecommunications companies for malicious purposes.

Chinese intelligence collection efforts against the U.S. government are growing in "scale, intensity and sophistication."[12] Chinese actors are also the world's most active and persistent perpetrators of economic espionage.[13] U.S. private sector firms and cyber-security specialists report an ongoing onslaught of sophisticated computer network intrusions that originate in China, and are almost certainly the work of, or have the backing of, the Chinese government.[14] Further, Chinese intelligence services, as well as private companies and other entities, often recruit those with direct access to corporate networks to steal trade secrets and other sensitive proprietary data.[15]

These cyber and human-enabled espionage efforts often exhibit sophisticated technological capabilities, and these capabilities have the potential to translate into efforts to insert malicious hardware or software implants into Chinese-manufactured telecommunications components and systems marketed to the United States. Opportunities to tamper with telecommunications components and systems are present throughout product development, and vertically integrated industry giants like Huawei and ZTE provide a wealth of opportunities for Chinese intelligence agencies to insert malicious hardware or software implants into critical telecommunications components and systems.[16] China may seek cooperation from the leadership of a company like Huawei or ZTE for these reasons. Even if the company's leadership refused such a request, Chinese intelligence services need only recruit working-level technicians or managers in these companies. Further, it appears that under Chinese law, ZTE and Huawei would be obligated to cooperate with any request by the Chinese government to use their systems or access them for malicious purposes under the guise of state security.[17]

A sophisticated nation-state actor like China has the motivation to tamper with the global telecommunications supply chain, with the United States being a significant priority. The ability to deny service or disrupt global systems allows a foreign entity the opportunity to exert pressure or control over critical infrastructure on which the country is dependent. The capacity to maliciously modify or steal information from government and corporate entities provides China access to expensive and time-consuming research and development that advances China's economic place in the world. Access to U.S. telecommunications infrastructure also allows China to engage in undetected espionage against the United States government and private sector interests.[18] China's military and intelligence services, recognizing the technological superiority of the U.S. military, are actively searching for asymmetrical advantages that could be exploited in any future conflict with the United States.[19] Inserting malicious hardware or software implants into Chinese-manufactured telecommunications components and systems headed for U.S. customers could allow Beijing to shut down or degrade critical national security systems in a time of crisis or war. Malicious implants in the components of critical infrastructure, such as power grids or financial networks, would also be a tremendous weapon in China's arsenal.

Malicious Chinese hardware or software implants would also be a potent espionage tool for penetrating sensitive U.S. national security systems, as well as providing access to the closed American corporate networks that contain the sensitive trade secrets, advanced research and development data, and negotiating or litigation positions that China would find useful in obtaining an unfair diplomatic or commercial advantage over the United States.

In addition to supply chain risks associated with hardware and software, managed services also pose a threat. Managed services, sold as part of the systems maintenance contract, allow for remote network access for everyday updates to software and patches to glitches. Unfortunately, such contracts may also allow the managed-service contractor to use its authorized access for malicious activity under the guise of legitimate assistance. Such access also offers an opportunity for more-tailored economic or state-sponsored espionage activities. Telecommunications companies such as Huawei are seeking to expand service portions of their business.[20]

The U.S. Government has acknowledged these concerns with telecommunications supply chain risk for several years. Indeed, as one of twelve critical infrastructure protection priorities outlined in the White House's 2009 Comprehensive National Cybersecurity Initiative (CNCI), Supply Chain Risk Management (SCRM) is identified as a national concern. Similarly, the Executive Branch continues to review supply chain issues consistent with its National Strategy for Global Supply Chain Security, released in January 2012. A key part of the management of supply chain risk, as explained in the report, is to properly "understand and identify vulnerabilities to the supply chain that stem from both exploitation of the system by those seeking to introduce harmful products or materials and disruptions from intentional attacks, accidents, or natural disasters."[21]

B. Suggested "mitigation measures" cannot fully address the threat posed by Chinese telecommunications companies providing equipment and services to United States critical infrastructure.

Many countries struggle with the potential threats posed by untrustworthy telecommunications companies. In Great Britain, the government took initial steps (as part of an overall mitigation strategy) to address its concerns by entering into an agreement with Huawei to establish an independently managed Cyber Security Evaluation Centre (CSEC). CSEC conducts independent reviews of Huawei's equipment and software deployed to the United Kingdom's telecommunications infrastructure, and provides such results to the relevant UK carriers and UK government. The goal of the British government is to attempt to lessen the threat that Huawei products deployed in critical UK telecommunications infrastructure pose to the availability or integrity of UK networks.

Huawei and ZTE have proposed similar schemes for products entering the United States market, administered without U.S. government involvement, but by Electronic Warfare Associates or other private-sector security firms.[22] These partnerships seek to address concerns that the companies could permit the Chinese government to insert features or vulnerabilities into their products, which would assist espionage or cyber warfare. Unfortunately, there are concerns that such efforts if taken in the United States will fall short of addressing security concerns given the breadth and scale of the U.S. telecommunications market.

Post-production evaluation processes are a standard approach to determining the security properties of complex, software-intensive systems. Processes like the Common Criteria for Information Technology Security Evaluation and various private certification services define a process by which an evaluator measures a product against a set of standards and assigns a security rating. The rating is meant to help a consumer know how much confidence to place in the security features of the device or software package. Both the implementation of the system and the methodology used to develop it, as documented by the manufacturer, are typically used as evidence for the chosen rating. Further, such processes are not necessarily designed to uncover malicious code but to encourage a foundational security baseline in security-enabled products.

For a variety of technical and economic reasons, evaluation programs as proposed by Huawei and ZTE are less useful than one might expect. In fact, the programs may create a false sense of security that an incomplete, flawed, or misapplied evaluation would provide. An otherwise careful consumer may choose to forego a thorough threat, application, and environment-based risk assessment, and the costs such evaluations entail, because an accredited outside expert has "blessed" the product in some way.

One key issue not addressed by standardized third-party security evaluations is product and deployment diversity. The behavior of a device or system can vary wildly depending on how and where it is configured, installed, and maintained. For time and cost reasons, an evaluation usually targets a snapshot of one product model configured in a specific and often unrealistically restrictive way. The pace of technology development today drives products to evolve far more rapidly than any third-party comprehensive evaluation process can follow. The narrow configuration specification used during testing almost ensures that an evaluated device will be deployed in a way not specifically covered by a formal evaluation. A security evaluation of a complex device is useless if the device is not deployed precisely in the same configuration as it was tested.

The evaluation of products prior to deployment only addresses the product portion of the lifecycle of networks. It is also important to recognize that how a network operator oversees its patch management, its trouble-shooting and maintenance, upgrades, and managed-service elements, as well as the vendors it chooses for such services, will affect the ongoing security of the network.

Vendors financing their own security evaluations create conflicts of interest that lead to skepticism about the independence and rigor of the result. A product manufacturer will naturally pursue its own interests and ends which are not necessarily aligned with all interests of the consumers. A different, but related, race to the bottom has been noted for the similarly vendor-financed Common Criteria evaluations.[23] The designers of the Common Criteria system understood this danger and implemented government certification for evaluators. The precaution seems mostly cosmetic as no certification has ever been challenged or revoked despite gaming and poor evaluation performance. Given similar concerns and about conflicts of interest, Huawei's U.K. evaluators of Huawei equipment have been vetted by the U.K. government and hold government security clearances, and the U.K. process has the support of the U.K. Carriers. It is not clear yet, however, that such steps would readily transfer to the U.S. market or successfully overcome the natural incentives of the situation and lead to truly independent investigations.

The task of finding and eliminating every significant vulnerability from a complex product is monumental. If we also consider flaws intentionally inserted by a determined and clever insider, the task becomes virtually impossible.[24] While there is a large body of literature describing techniques for finding latent vulnerabilities in hardware and software systems, no such technique claims the ability to find all such vulnerabilities in a pre-existing system. Techniques do exist that can prove a system implementation matches a design which has been formally verified to be free of certain types of flaws.[25] However, such formal techniques must be incorporated throughout the design and development process to be effective. They cannot currently be applied to a finished product of significant size or complexity. Even when embedded into a design and development process, formal techniques of this type do not yet scale to the size of complete commercial telecommunication systems. It is highly unlikely that a security evaluation partnership such as that proposed by Huawei or ZTE, independent of its competence and motives, will be able to identify all relevant flaws in products the size and complexity of core network infrastructure devices. If significant flaws remain in widely fielded products and processes that are known to a potential adversary, it seems like the evaluation process has provided only marginal benefit.

A security evaluation of potentially suspect equipment being deployed in critical infrastructure roles may seem like an answer to the security problems posed. Unfortunately, given the complexity of the telecommunications grid, the limitations of current security evaluation techniques, and the economics of vendor-financed analyses provide a sense of security but not actual security. Significant security is available only through a thoughtful design and engineering process that addresses a complete system-of-systems across its full lifecycle, from design to retirement and includes aspects such as discrete technology components, their interactions, the human environment, and threats from the full spectrum of adversaries. The result of such a process should be a convincing set of diverse evidence that a system is worthy of our trust.[26]

II. Investigation

A. Scope of Investigation

The House Permanent Select Committee on Intelligence is responsible for authorizing the intelligence activities of the United States and overseeing those activities to ensure that they are legal, effective, and properly resourced to protect the national security interests of the United States. Specifically, the Committee is charged with reviewing and studying on a continuing basis the authorities, programs, and activities of the Intelligence Community and with reviewing and studying on an exclusive basis the sources and methods of the community.[27] Along with this responsibility is the obligation to study and understand the range of foreign threats faced by the United States, including those directed against our nation's critical infrastructure. Similarly, the Committee must evaluate the threats from foreign intelligence operations and ensure that the country's counterintelligence agencies are appropriately focused on and resourced to defeat those operations.[28]

The Committee's goals in this investigation were to inquire into the potential security risk posed by the top two Chinese telecommunications companies and review whether our government is properly positioned to understand and respond to that threat. An additional aim of this process has been to determine what information could be provided in an unclassified form to shed light on the key questions of whether the existence of these firms in our market would pose a national-security risk through the potential loss of control of U.S. critical infrastructure.

Of course, the United States' telecommunications sector increasingly relies on a global supply chain for the production and delivery of equipment and services. That reliance presents significant risks that other individuals or entities – including those backed by foreign governments – can and will exploit and undermine the reliability of the networks. Better understanding the supply-chain risks we face is vital if we are to protect the security and functionality of our networks and if we are to guard against national security and economic threats to those networks. The investigation's scope reflects the underlying need for the U.S. to manage the global supply chain system using a risk-based approach.

Recent studies highlight that actors in China are the source of more cyber-attacks than in any other country. The National Counterintelligence Executive, for example, explained, in an open report on cyber-espionage, that "Chinese actors are the world's most active and persistent perpetrators of economic espionage."[29] Thus, the Committee focused on those companies with the strongest potential Chinese ties and those that also seek greater entry into the United States market. Both Huawei and ZTE are indigenous Chinese firms, with histories that include connections to the Chinese government. Both Huawei and ZTE have already incorporated United States' subsidiaries, and both are seeking to expand their footprint in the United States market. Huawei has received, thus far, the greatest attention from analysts and the media. Given the similarities of the two companies, however, including their potential ties to the Chinese government, support by the Chinese government, and goals to further their U.S. presence, the Committee focused on both Huawei and ZTE.

Both Huawei and ZTE assert that the Committee should not focus only on them to the exclusion of all other companies that manufacture parts or equipment in China. The Committee recognizes that many non-Chinese companies, including U.S. technology companies, manufacture some of their products in China. But it is not only the location of manufacturing that is important to the risk calculation. It is also ownership, history, and the products being marketed. These may not be the only two companies presenting this risk, but they are the two largest Chinese-founded, Chinese-owned telecommunications companies seeking to market critical network equipment to the United States. To review supply chain risk, the Committee decided to focus first on the largest perceived vulnerabilities, with an expectation that the conclusion of this investigation would inform how to view the potential threat to the supply chain from other companies or manufacturers operating in China and other countries.

B. Investigative Process

The Committee's investigative process included extensive interviews with company and government officials, numerous document requests, and an open hearing with a senior official from both Huawei and ZTE. Committee staff reviewed available information on the specific companies, and Committee staff and members met with Huawei and ZTE officials for lengthy, in-depth meetings and interviews. Committee staff also toured the companies' facilities and factories.

Specifically, on February 23, 2012, Committee staff met with and interviewed corporate executives of Huawei at its corporate headquarters in Shenzhen, China. The delegation toured Huawei's corporate headquarters, reviewed company product lines, and toured a large manufacturing factory. Officials involved in the discussion from Huawei included Ken Hu, Huawei's Deputy Chairman of the Board and Acting CEO; Evan Bai,

Vice President of the Treasury Management Office; Charlie Chen, Senior Vice President in charge of Huawei (USA); Jiang Xisheng, Secretary of the Board; John Suffolk, Global Security Officer; and Rose Hao, Export Regulator.

On April 12, 2012, Committee staff met with and interviewed corporate executives of ZTE at its corporate headquarters in Shenzhen, China. In addition to these meetings, the delegation took a brief tour of ZTE's corporate headquarters, including a factory site. Officials from ZTE included Zhu Jinyun, ZTE's Senior Vice President, U.S. and North America Market; Fan Qingfeng, Executive Vice President of Global Marketing and Sales; Guo Jianjun, Legal Director; Timothy Steinert, Independent Director of the Board (and Ali Baba Counsel); Ma Xuexing, Legal Director; Cao Wei, Security and Investor Relations with the Information Disclosure Office; Qian Yu, Security and Investor Relations with the Information Disclosure Office; and John Merrigan, attorney with DLA Piper.

In May of 2012, Ranking Member Ruppersberger along with Committee members Representative Nunes, Representative Bachmann, and Representative Schiff traveled to Hong Kong to meet with senior officials of both Huawei and ZTE. In addition to the senior officials present at the staff meetings, the Committee members met with Ren Zhengfei, the founder and President of Huawei.

After the meetings, the Committee followed-up with several pages of written questions and document requests to fill in information gaps, inconsistent or incomplete answers, and the need for corroborating documentary evidence of many of the companies' factual and historical assertions. Unfortunately, neither company was completely or fully responsive to the Committee's document requests. Indeed, neither Huawei nor ZTE provided internal documents in response to the Committee's letter.[30] To attempt, again, to answer the remaining questions, the Committee called each company to an open hearing.

On September 13, 2012, the Committee held an open hearing with representatives of both ZTE and Huawei. The witnesses included Mr. Charles Ding, corporate senior vice president and Huawei's representative to the United States, and Mr. Zhu Jinyun, ZTE senior vice president for North America and Europe. The hearing was designed to be both thorough and fair. The witnesses were each given twenty minutes for an opening statement and each was aided by an interpreter during the question and answer portion of the hearing to ensure that the witnesses were given the maximum opportunity to understand the questions and answer completely and factually.[31]

Once again, the witnesses' answers were often vague and incomplete. For example, they claimed to have no understanding or knowledge of commonly used terms, could not answer questions about the composition of their internal Party Committees, refused to provide straightforward answers about their operations in the United States, sought to avoid answering questions about their histories of intellectual property protection, and claimed to have no understanding or knowledge of Chinese laws that force them to comply with the Chinese government's requests for access to their equipment. The companies' responses to the Committee's questions for the record after the hearing included similar evasive answers.

C. Investigative Challenges

This unclassified report discloses the unclassified information the Committee received when trying to understand the nature of these companies, the formal role of the Chinese government or Chinese Communist Party within them, and their current operations in the United States. In pursuing this goal, the Committee faced many challenges, some of which are shared by many who seek to understand the relationship between the government and business in China and the threat posed to our infrastructure. These challenges include: the lack of transparency in Chinese corporate and bureaucratic structures that leads to a lack of trust; general private sector concerns with providing proprietary or confidential information; fears of retribution if private-sector companies or individuals discuss their concerns; and uncertain attribution of cyber attacks.

The classified annex provides significantly more information adding to the Committee's concerns. That information cannot be shared publicly without risking U.S. national security. The unclassified report itself, however, highlights that Huawei and ZTE have failed to assuage the Committee's significant security concerns presented by their continued expansion into the United States. Indeed, given the companies' repeated failure to answer key questions thoroughly and clearly, or support those answers with credible internal evidence, the national-security concerns about their operations have not been ameliorated. In fact, given their obstructionist behavior, the Committee believes addressing these concerns have become an imperative for the country.

In addition to the Committee's discussions with the companies, the Committee investigators spoke with industry experts and former and present employees about the companies. Companies around the United States have experienced odd or alerting incidents using Huawei or ZTE equipment. Officials with these companies, however, often expressed concern that publicly acknowledging these incidents would be detrimental to their internal investigations and attribution efforts, undermine their ongoing efforts to defend their systems, and also put at risk their ongoing contracts.

Similarly, statements by former or current employees describing flaws in the Huawei or ZTE equipment and other potentially unethical or illegal behavior by Huawei officials were hindered by employees' fears of retribution or retaliation.[32]

Further, the inherent difficulty in attributing the precise individual or entity responsible for known attacks within the United States continues to hinder the technological capability for investigators to determine the source of attacks or any connections among industry, government, and the hacker community within China.[33]

III. Summary of Findings

Chinese telecommunications companies provide an opportunity for the Chinese government to tamper with the United States telecommunications supply chain. That said, understanding the level and means of state influence and control of economic entities in China remains difficult. As Chinese analysts explain, state control or influence of purportedly private-sector entities in China is neither clear nor disclosed.[34] The Chinese government and the Chinese Communist Party, experts explain, can exert influence over the corporate boards and management of private sector companies, either formally through personnel choices, or in more subtle ways.[35] As ZTE's submission to the Committee states, "the degree of possible government influence must vary across a spectrum."[36]

The Committee thus focused primarily on reviewing Huawei's and ZTE's ties to the Chinese state, including support by the Chinese government and state-owned banks, their connections to the Chinese Communist Party, and their work done on behalf of the Chinese military and intelligence services. The Committee also probed the companies' compliance with U.S. laws, such as those protecting intellectual property, to determine whether the companies can be trusted as good corporate actors. The Committee did not attempt a review of all technological vulnerabilities of particular ZTE and Huawei products or components. Of course, the Committee took seriously recent allegations of backdoors, or other unexpected elements in either company's products, as reported previously and during the course of the investigation. But the expertise of the Committee does not lend itself to comprehensive reviews of particular pieces of equipment.

The investigation sought to answer several key questions about the companies that would, including:

- What are the companies' histories and management structures, including any initial ties to the Chinese government, military, or Communist party?

11

- How and to what extent does the Chinese government or the Chinese Communist Party exert control or influence over the decisions, operations, and strategy of Huawei and ZTE?
- Are Huawei and ZTE treated as national champions or otherwise given unfair or special advantages or financial incentives by the Chinese government?
- What is the presence of each company in the United States market and how much influence does the parent company in Shenzhen influence its operations in the United States?
- Do the companies comply with legal obligations, including those protecting intellectual property rights and international sanctions regimes (such as those with respect to Iran)?

The Committee found the companies' responses to these lines of inquiry inadequate and unclear. Moreover, despite repeated requests, the companies' consistently provided very little – if any – internal documentation substantiating their answers. The few documents provided could rarely be authenticated or validated because of the companies' failure to follow standard document-production standards as provided by the Committee and standard with such investigations. Moreover, the apparent control of the Chinese government over this information remains a hindrance to a thorough investigation. One of the companies asserted clearly both verbally and in writing that it could not provide internal documentation that was not first approved by the Chinese government.[37] The fact that Chinese companies believe that their internal documentation or information remains a "state secret," only heightens concerns about Chinese government control over these firms and their operations.

The Committee is disappointed that Huawei and ZTE neither answered fully nor chose to provide supporting documentation for their claims, especially given that Huawei requested a thorough and complete investigation. The Committee simply cannot rely on the statements of company officials that their equipment's presence in U.S. critical infrastructure does not present a threat, and that the companies are not, or would not be, under pressure by the Chinese government to act in ways contrary to United States interests. The findings below summarize what the Committee has learned from information available, and suggest avenues for further inquiry.

A. The Committee finds that Huawei did not fully cooperate with the investigation and was unwilling to explain its relationship with the Chinese government or Chinese Communist Party, while credible evidence exists that it fails to comply with U.S. laws.

Throughout this investigation, Huawei officials sought to portray the company as transparent. Huawei consistently refused, however, to provide detailed answers in written form or provide internal documentation to support their answers to questions at the heart of the investigation. Specifically, Huawei would not fully describe the history, structure, and management of Huawei and its subsidiaries to the Committee's satisfaction. The Committee received almost no information on the role of Chinese Communist Party Committee within Huawei or specifics about how Huawei interacts in formal channels with the Chinese government. Huawei refused to provide details about its business operations in the United States, failed to disclose details of its dealings with the Chinese military or intelligence services, and would not provide clear answers on the firm's decision-making processes. Huawei also failed to provide any internal documents in response to the Committee's written document requests, thus impeding the Committee's ability to evaluate fully the company's answers or claims.

In addition to discussions with Huawei officials, the Committee has interviewed several current and former employees of Huawei USA, whose employees describe a company that is managed almost completely by the Huawei parent company in China, thus undermining Huawei's claims that its United States operations are largely independent of parent company. The testimony and evidence of individuals who currently or formerly worked for Huawei in the United States or who have done business with Huawei also brought to light several very serious allegations of illegal behavior that require additional investigation. The Committee will refer these matters to the Executive Branch for potential investigation.

These allegations were not the focus or thrust of the investigation, but they were uncovered in the course of the investigation. The Committee believes that they reveal a potential pattern of unethical and illegal behavior by Huawei officials, allegations that of themselves create serious doubts about whether Huawei can be trusted to operate in the United States in accordance with United States legal requirements and international codes of business conduct.

i. **Huawei did not provide clear and complete information on its corporate structure and decision-making processes, and it likely remains dependent on the Chinese government for support.**

Huawei markets itself as a "leading global ICT ["Information Communications Technology"] solution provider," that is "committed to providing reliable and secure networks."[38] Throughout the investigation, Huawei consistently denied having any links to the Chinese government and maintains that it is a private, employee-owned company.[39] Many industry analysts, however, have suggested otherwise; many believe, for example, that the founder of Huawei, Ren Zhengfei, was a director of the People's Liberation

13

Army (PLA) Information Engineering Academy, an organization that they believe is associated with 3PLA, China's signals intelligence division, and that his connections to the military continue.[40] Further, many analysts suggest that the Chinese government and military proclaim that Huawei is a "national champion" and provide Huawei market-distorting financial support.[41]

In seeking to understand the Chinese government's influence or control over Chinese telecommunications companies, the Committee focused on Huawei's corporate structure and decision-making processes. Better information about Huawei's corporate structure would also help answer lingering questions caused by Huawei's historic lack of transparency.[42] For years, analysts have struggled to understand how Huawei's purported employee-ownership model works in practice, and how that ownership translates into corporate leadership and decision-making.[43] Huawei repeatedly asserts that it is a private, employee-owned and controlled company that is not influenced by the Chinese government or Chinese Communist Party.[44] Executives also asserted that the unique shareholder and compensation arrangement is the foundation of the company's rise and success.

Available information does not align with Huawei's description of this structure, and many analysts believe that Huawei is not actually controlled by its common shareholders, but actually controlled by an elite subset of its management.[45] The Committee thus requested further information on the structure of the company's ownership. For example, the Committee requested that Huawei list the ten largest shareholders of the company. Huawei refused to answer.[46] At the hearing on September 13, 2012, Huawei admits that its shareholder agreement gives veto power to Ren Zhengfei, the founder and president of the company.[47] Other public statements by the company undermine the suggestion that the 60,000 supposed shareholders of Huawei control the company's decisions. For example, in the company's 2011 report, Mr. Ren highlighted that Huawei's Board of Directors:

> will not make maximizing the interests of stakeholders (including employees, governments, and suppliers) its goal. Rather, it holds on to the core corporate values that are centered on customer interests and encourage employee dedication.[48]

Such statements undermine the credibility of Huawei's repeated claims that its employees control the company. Thus, to explore these conflicts, the Committee focused much attention on the shareholder program. Of note, the only nonpublic, purportedly internal documents that Huawei provided to the Committee in the course of the investigation are unsigned copies of its shareholder agreement documents. Unfortunately, the Committee could not verify the legitimacy of these documents, because they were unsigned and non-official.

Huawei officials explained that Chinese law forbids foreigners from holding shares in Chinese companies absent a special waiver.[49] Current and former Huawei employees confirm that only Chinese nationals working at Huawei in the United States participate in the shareholding plan. The inability of non-Chinese employees of Huawei to hold shares of the company further erodes its claim that it is truly an employee-run organization as an entire group of employees are not only disadvantaged, but automatically excluded from any chance to participate in the process.

Huawei consistently asserted that the Chinese government has no influence over corporate behavior and that the company is instead managed as an employee-owned enterprise through Huawei's Employee Stock Ownership Program (ESOP). Officials explained that the shareholding plan is not a benefits plan; rather, it provides high-performing employees an option to buy dividend-providing shares and thereby share in the value of the company. Eligible employees are given the option to buy shares at a certain company determined price, and can only sell the shares when they leave the company or with approval.[50]

Huawei also provided staff access to shareholder ballots for shareholder representatives and the Board of Directors. These too did not appear to be facially fraudulent, but they were impossible to authenticate, especially as investigators were not allowed to remove the documents from Huawei's facilities for third-party validation. The documents appeared to highlight that shareholders have a write-in option for union representatives, but there is no such option for the Board of Directors. Rather, Huawei officials stated that the nominees for the Board are chosen prior to the vote by the previous Board. It was unclear how the original Board was established, and Huawei has consistently failed to provide any answers about who was previously on its Board of Directors.

Huawei further explained that in 1994, the first Company Law of China was officially published, regulating the establishment and operations of limited liability companies.[51] Under this law, the maximum number of shareholders was 50 individuals. Thus, in 1997, Huawei claims to have changed its legal structure to a limited liability company, and started the employee stock ownership program through the union. Similarly, Huawei asserted that in 1997, the City of Shenzhen issued policies regarding employee shareholdings. According to Huawei, it designed its shareholder program to conform to the the Company Law of China, and the laws and policies of the City of Shenzhen.[52]

According to Huawei, the union, known as Union of Huawei Investment and Holding Co., Ltd., facilitates ESOP implementation. The Union is a lawfully registered association of China. Huawei officials stated that "Huawei's success can be directly linked to the company's unique compensation structure."[53] Currently, Huawei claims that the Union holds 98.7% of the ESOP shares, and Mr. Ren holds 1.3%. At the Huawei explained that as of December 31, 2011, ESOP has 65,596 participants, which it alleges are all Huawei employees (current and retired), it claims that there are no third parties, including government institutions, holding any ownership-stake in the company.

Questions remained after the Committee staff's meeting with Huawei officials. Most importantly, the Committee did not receive clear information about how precisely candidates for the Board of Directors are chosen. This is a concern because such individuals are key decision-makers of the company and those whose potential connections to the government are of high concern. According to Huawei officials, the previous Board nominates the individuals for the current Board. But it is not clear how the original Board was established and Huawei refuses to describe how the first Board of Directors and first Supervisory Board were chosen.[54]

As described above, Huawei provided the Committee unsigned, unauthenticated documents purporting to be: (1) Articles of Restricted Phantom Shares; (2) Letter of Undertakings of Restricted Phantom Shares; (3) Notice of Share Issuance and Confirmation Letter; (4) List of Shareholding Employees; (5) Record of Employee Payments and Buyback, (6) Receipts of Employee Share Payments and Buyback; (7) Election Records of the 2010 ESOP Representatives Election (procedures, ballots, results, announcements, etc.); (8) and conclusions of the 2010 ESOP Representatives Meeting. The Committee could not validate the legitimacy of these documents given that Huawei only provided unsigned drafts. Below are summaries of key information from these documents.[55]

(1) ESOP Restricted Phantom Shares--Summary

- ESOP Restricted Phantom Shares Article 20 states that target grantees of employee stocks are current employees with high performance.

16

- Each year, the company determines the numbers of shares an employee can purchase based on job performance. Eligible employees must sign the Confirmation Letter and the Letter of Undertakings and make payments for the shares.

- An employee's stocks can be held only by the employee him/herself, and cannot be transferred or disposed by the employee. When an employee leaves the company (except for those who meet the retirement requirements with minimal eight years of tenure and 45 years old), stocks will be purchased back by the company.

- The current stock price is the net asset value of the stock from the previous year. When an employee purchases more shares or the Union takes shares back, it is based on the current stock price. The dividend amount of each year is based on the performance of the company.

(2) Articles of Restricted Phantom Shares—

  a. The Commission

- The Commission is composed of 51 Representatives and nine alternates, elected by the Active Beneficiaries as organized by the Union with a term of five years.

  - Active beneficiary is defined as an active employee who works at Shenzhen Huawei Investment and Holding Co, Ltd or any of its equity affiliates and participates in the Plan of the Union.

  - In the event there is a vacancy, the Alternate shall take up the vacancy in sequence. The Alternates can attend, but not vote at, all meetings.

  - The Commission reviews and approves restricted phantom share issuance proposals; reviews and approves dividend distribution proposals; reviews and approves reports of the board of shareholding employees; elects and replaces any member of the board; elects and replaces any member of Supervisory Board; reviews and approves procedures for electing representatives; approves amendments of these articles; reviews and approves the use of the reserve fund; reviews and approves other material matters with respect to restricted phantom share; perform functions as the shareholders of the company, exercises the rights of the shareholder, and develops resolutions regarding material matters such as capital increase, profit distribution, and selection of Directors and Supervisors.

- Meetings of the Commission shall be convened at least once a year, and shall be convened by the Board and presided over by the Chairman of the Board or the Vice Chairman.

b. The Board

- The Board is responsible for regular management authority and shall be responsible to the Commission.

- The main functions of the Board are to: prepare restricted phantom share issuance proposal; preparation of the dividends distribution proposal; formulation, approval, and amendment of the detailed rules, processes, and implementation methods with respect to the restricted phantom shares; preparation of the amendments to articles; determination on the detailed proposal as to the use of the Reserve Fund; execution of the resolutions of the Commission; exercise of the specific rights and powers of a shareholder of the Investee Company except for the matters on which a resolution from Commission is required; determination of other matters that shall be determined by the Board.

- The Board consists of 13 directors selected by the Commission; each serves for five years.

- The Board must convene at least once a year; it needs 2/3 present, and resolutions of the meetings shall be approved by at least 1/2 of all Directors.

- The Board may establish a restricted phantom share management committee and other necessary organizations responsible for carrying out and implementing the work assigned by the Board and for detailed matters with respect to the management of the restricted phantom shares, such as evaluation, distribution, and repurchase of the restricted phantom shares as well as management of the account and the Reserve Fund/treasury shares related to restricted phantom shares.

c. *Supervisory Board*

- The Supervisory Board is the organization responsible for supervising the implementation of the shareholder plan with its main functions and powers as follows:
  - supervising the implementation of the resolutions by the Board;
  - making recommendations or inquiries in event of any violation of any law, regulation or these Articles by the Board;
  - making work reports to the Commission; and
  - other regular functions and powers.

- Supervisors may attend Board meetings as non-voting delegate.

- The Supervisory Board shall consist of five Supervisors who shall be elected by the Commission to five year terms; no Director can serve concurrently as a Supervisor.

- Convene at least once a year, need minimum of 2/3 present, resolutions require approval of at least 2/3 of all Supervisors

d. *Validity of Resolutions*

- Before 31 December 2018, Mr. Ren shall have a right to veto the decisions regarding restricted phantom shares and Huawei's material matters (resolutions of the Board, Commission, and Shareholder's Meeting of the Company).

- Starting from 1 January 2013, the confirmed Active Beneficiaries who represent a minimum of 15% of the restricted phantom shares (excluding the restricted phantom shares held by the Restructuring Beneficiaries and the Retained Restricted Phantom Shares) shall have a right to veto the decisions regarding restricted phantom shares and Huawei's material matters (including resolutions of the Board, the Commission, and the Shareholders' Meeting of the Company).

- The relevant resolutions shall take effect in the event that the owner(s) of the right of veto does (do) not exercise the right of veto against the aforementioned resolutions.

(3) Acquisition of Restricted Phantom Shares

- The restricted phantom shares of the Union shall be issued to those key employees of the Company who have displayed excellent work performance.

- The Restricted Phantom Share Management Committee shall decide annually whether to issue shares, and the number of shares to be issued, based on the comprehensive evaluation of the work performance of such employee and in accordance with the evaluation rules of the restricted phantom shares. Retired or restructuring beneficiaries are not allowed to purchase new shares.

(4) Confidentiality and Non-Competition Obligations of the Beneficiaries

- No Active Beneficiary or Restructuring Beneficiary shall directly or indirectly have a second job in any way, work for any enterprise other than the Company without written consent of the Company or without entering into the relevant agreement with the Company.

****

20

ii. Huawei failed to explain its relationships with the Chinese government, and its assertions denying support by the Chinese government are not credible.

The nature of the modern Chinese economy is relevant for understanding Huawei's connection to the Chinese state. The Chinese government often provides financial backing to industries and companies of strategic importance. Indeed, analysts of the Chinese political economy state that:

> Huawei operates in what Beijing explicitly refers to as one of seven "strategic sectors." Strategic sectors are those considered as core to the national and security interests of the state. In these sectors, the CCP [Chinese Communist Party] ensures that "national champions" dominate through a combination of market protectionism, cheap loans, tax and subsidy programs, and diplomatic support in the case of offshore markets. Indeed, it is not possible to thrive in one of China's strategic sectors without regime largesse and approval.[56]

Similarly, the U.S.-China Commission has explained, with Chinese companies, "the government's role is not always straightforward or disclosed." Despite some reforms, "much of the Chinese economy remains under the ownership or control of various parts of the Chinese government."[57] The U.S. China-Commission lists Huawei as a form of enterprise in China that exists in a relatively new market and receives generous government policies to support its development and impose difficulties for foreign competition.[58]

The Committee thus inquired into the precise relationship between the Chinese government and Huawei. During the Committee's meetings with Huawei executives, and during the open hearing on September 13, 2012, Huawei officials consistently denied having any connection to or influence by the Chinese government beyond that which is typical regulation.[59] Specifically, Huawei explained in its written responses to the Committee, that "Huawei maintains normal commercial communication and interaction with relevant government supervisory agencies, including the Ministry of Industry and Information Technology and the Ministry of Commerce."[60] Huawei claims that it "does not interact with government agencies that are not relevant to its business activities, including the Ministry of National Defense, the Ministry of State Security, and the Central Military Commission."[61] Huawei, however, did not provide information with which the Committee could evaluate these claims, as Huawei refused to answer the specific questions of the Committee inquiring about the company's precise mechanisms of interaction with and regulation by these government bodies.

The Committee did not expect Huawei to prove that it has "no ties" to the government. Rather, in light of even experts' lack of certainty about the state-run capitalist system in China, the Committee sought greater understanding of its actual relationship with the Chinese government. The Committee requested that Huawei support and prove its statements about its regulatory interaction by providing details and evidence explaining the nature of this formal interaction. Any company operating in the United States could very easily describe and produce evidence of the federal entities with which it must interact, including which government officials are their main points of contact at those regulatory agencies.

In its written submission in response to the Committee's questions, Huawei simply asserted that it "maintains normal commercial communication and interaction with relevant government supervisory agencies, including the Ministry of Industry and Information Technology and the Ministry of Commerce."[62] Huawei's failure to provide further detailed information explaining how it is formally regulated, controlled, or otherwise managed by the Chinese government undermines the company's repeated assertions that it is not inappropriately influenced by the Chinese government. Huawei appears simply unwilling to provide greater details that would explain its relationships with the Chinese government in a way that would alleviate security concerns.

Similarly, Huawei officials did not provide detailed answers about the backgrounds of *previous* Board Members. Rather, the Committee simply received the same biographies as previously disclosed of current members of the Board of Directors and Supervisory Board.[63] Previous Board Members may have significant ties to the Party, military, or government. And since the previous Board is responsible for nominating the current Board members, this information is important to understanding the historical progression of the company. Because the biographies of the previous members would highlight possible connections to military or intelligence elements of the Chinese government, Huawei's consistent failure to provide this information is alerting.

iii. **Huawei admits that the Chinese Communist Party maintains a Party Committee within the company, but it failed to explain what that Committee does on behalf of the Party or which individuals compose the Committee.**

Huawei's connection to the Chinese Communist Party is a key concern for the Committee because it represents the opportunity for the State to exert its influence over the decisions and operations of a company seeking to expand into the critical infrastructure in the United States. This concern is founded on the ubiquitous nature of the Chinese Party in the affairs of institutions and entities in China, and the consensus view that the Party exerts pressure on and directs the resources of economic actors in China.[64]

In response to the numerous opportunities to answer questions about its connection to the Party, Huawei stated that the company has no relevant connections. For example, in response to the Committee's written questions about the role of the Party in the company's affairs, Huawei merely stated that it "has no relationship with the Chinese Communist Party in its *business* activities."[65]

Huawei admits, however, that an internal Party Committee exists within Huawei. Huawei simply states that party committees are required by Chinese law to exist in all companies in China.[66] The existence of these Committees is, however, of particular relevance. Huawei states in its defense that all economic institutions in China are required to have a state Party apparatus inside the company. This is not, however, a compelling defense for companies seeking to build critical infrastructure in the United States. Indeed, experts in Chinese political economy agree that it is through these Committees that the Party exerts influence, pressure, and monitoring of corporate activities. In essence, these Committees provide a shadow source of power and influence directing, even in subtle ways, the direction and movement of economic resources in China.[67] It is therefore suspicious that Huawei refuses to discuss or describe that Party Committee's membership. Huawei similarly refuses to explain what decisions of the company are reviewed by the Party Committee, and how individuals are chosen to serve on the Party Committee.

Similarly, Huawei officials did not provide information about Mr. Ren's role or stature in the Party. In his official biography, Mr. Ren admits that he was asked to be a member of the 12th National Congress of the Communist Party of China in 1982. The National Congress is the once-in-a-decade forum through which the next leaders of the Chinese state are chosen. The Party members asked to play a role in China's leadership transition are considered key players in the state apparatus.[68] Mr. Ren proudly admits that he was invited to that Congress, but he will not describe his duties. Shortly after being given such a prestigious role, Mr. Ren successfully founded Huawei, though he asserts he did so without any government or Party assistance.[69] Huawei likewise refuses to answer whether Mr. Ren has been invited to subsequent National Congresses or has played any role in Party functions since that time.[70]

From the review of available information, Huawei may have connections and ties to Chinese leadership that it refuses to disclose. In light of Huawei's refusal to discuss details of its acknowledged Chinese Communist Party Committee, the Committee questions the company's ability to be candid about any other possible connections to the government, military, or Chinese Communist Party.

iv. Huawei's corporate history suggests ties to the Chinese military, and Huawei failed to provide detailed answers to questions about those connections.

Huawei explained the founding and development of the company by focusing on the life and history of Ren Zhengfei, Huawei's founder. According to Huawei officials, Mr. Ren was a member of the Chinese military's engineering corps as a soldier tasked to establish the Liao Yang Chemical Fiber Factory and was promoted as a Deputy Director, which was a professional role equivalent to a Deputy Regimental Chief, but without military rank.[71] Mr. Ren then retired from the army in 1983 after the engineering corps disbanded, and next worked for a State Owned Enterprise (SOE) following his retirement. According to this account, Mr. Ren was "dissatisfied" with his low salary and career path at the SOE, so in 1987, he established Huawei. Huawei officials did not explain how he was able to leave his employment with a SOE or whether he got agreement of the state to do so. Huawei officials denied that Mr. Ren was a senior member of the military.[72] The Committee's requests for more information about Mr. Ren's military and professional background were unanswered. Huawei refused to describe Mr. Ren's full military background. Huawei refused to state to whom he reported when he was in the military. Huawei refused to answer questions about how he was invited to join the 12th National Congress, what duties he performed for the Party, and whether he has been asked to similar state-party matters.

Huawei similarly denied allegations that Ms. Sun Yafang, Chairwoman of Huawei, was previously affiliated with the Ministry of State Security. Mr. Ding responded to Committee questions after the hearing that, to his knowledge, reports about Ms. Yafang in Chinese publications, such as those in *Xinjing Bao*, are erroneous.[73] Mr. Ding did not respond to questions asking about how such publications received such information, or whether Ms. Yafang's previous biography on the Huawei website was erroneous as well. Rather, Mr. Ding simply provided again Ms. Yafang's corporate biography from the Huawei Annual Report 2011.[74]

With respect to Huawei's founders, Huawei cited a Chinese legal requirement that new companies in the economic development zone must have a minimum of five shareholders and 20,000 RMB registered capital. During meetings with the Committee, Huawei officials claimed that in 1987, Mr. Ren raised 21,000 RMB with personal savings and five other private investors. To the best of the officials' knowledge, none of the five investors had worked with Mr. Ren prior to start-up and one individual has previous affiliation with the government.[75] According to Huawei officials, the five investors never actually worked for Huawei and withdrew their investments several years later.[76]

The Committee struggled to get answers from Huawei on the details of this founding, including how Mr. Ren came to know the initial individual investors, whether his connections to the military were important to the eventual development of the firm, and whether his role in the Party remains a factor in his and his company's success.

v.   **The Committee finds that Huawei's failure to provide information about the Chinese government's 1999 investigation of the company for tax fraud exemplifies how it refuses to be transparent; the apparent ease with which Huawei ended the investigation undermines Huawei's assertion that the Chinese government finds Huawei to be a disfavored telecommunications solutions provider in China.**

Huawei officials claimed that after growing in rural areas in China throughout the 1990s, the Chinese government investigated the company at length between 1998-99 for tax fraud.[77] Huawei officials stated that they believed this investigation was politically motivated and performed at the urging of the company's competition – specifically, other telecommunications companies that are also state-owned enterprises. Mr. Ken Hu explained the investigation was a turning point in the history of the company. Specifically, Mr. Hu stated that Huawei's movement to opportunities outside of China was the result of this investigation.[78] Indeed, these officials sought to explain that this episode proves that Huawei was not in fact a "national champion" or otherwise a favored company in China.[79]

Given the obvious importance Huawei placed on this tax-fraud investigation, the Committee's subsequent questions and document requests sought detailed information and further documentary support for its version of events. In particular, the Committee sought information on the conclusion of the Chinese investigation. This information is particularly important to the Committee given the apparent pride displayed by certain Huawei officials in Shenzhen when describing how they successfully used their connections to end the investigation. The ability of these corporate officers to end a politically-motivated investigation suggests that Huawei officials were not as lacking in political power or influence with the government as they suggested.

25

Despite the importance placed on this event, Huawei failed to address the Committee's questions in its written submission.[80]   The company also failed to provide any material that would support Huawei's assertions that the investigation was closed legitimately or without attendant conditions placed on Huawei.[81]

vi.   Huawei failed to explain its relationships with western consulting firms, and any claims that its success is on account of those relationships, rather than support by the Chinese government, are not credible.

Huawei officials stated that one reason for the company's success was its reliance on the advice of western consulting firms, such as IBM, Accenture, and Price Waterhouse Cooper.[82]   Huawei sought to convince the Committee that it was the advice of these companies -- and not support by the Chinese government -- that explains Huawei's miraculous growth in recent years.[83]

Because of the importance Huawei places on the advice given by these consulting firms, the Committee sought greater information and evidence showing that such advice had important effects for the company. The Committee made clear that it did not seek information on the terms of the contractual arrangements with the consulting firms, but rather what information they reviewed from Huawei and what advice was provided. The Committee offered to keep such information confidential to avoid concerns about disclosing proprietary information.

Huawei responded with only a vague description of the advice provided by these companies. Specifically, although "[s]ince 1997, Huawei has relied on western management consulting firms to help improve [its] capabilities, build [its] processes, and develop a comprehensive management system driven by customer requirements," Huawei failed to provide details about how those companies reformed the company other than providing a few sentences mentioning standard business practices, including lead to cash (LTC), integrated product development (IPD), issue to resolution (ITR), and integrated financial services (IFS). Huawei, refused "to provide additional details as to [its] consultancy relationships" citing concerns about proprietary information contained in that advice.[84] The Committee explained that it is most interested in evidence revealing what Huawei did in response to the advice of these firms, and specifically financial or other evidence that supports its position that those changes were responsible for efficiencies, growth, and market success.[85] Huawei could have answered such questions without revealing proprietary information held by these companies.[86] The Committee was also willing to enter into a confidentiality agreement with all parties, an offer Huawei declined to accept or pursue.[87]

Huawei has made the details of this consulting advice relevant to this investigation by attributing its rapid success to the advice rendered by these consulting firms. It is not then reasonable for Huawei to withhold that information from the Committee so that it could evaluate those claims. If Huawei has within its possession information and documents that would prove that the advice given by these firms was key to Huawei's success, Huawei should provide such information.[88] The Committee was and remains willing to enter into confidentiality agreements with all parties to solve any concerns about the release of proprietary information. Huawei has failed to accept this offer. Its failure to do so is indicative of the lack of cooperation shown throughout this investigation.

> **vii.   Huawei failed to answer key questions or provide supporting documentation for its claims to be financially independent of the Chinese government.**

As a company of strategic importance to China, Huawei's stature will be reflected in the level of financial support and direction it receives from the Chinese government and Party.[89] One way to review that support and direction provided by the state is through the financing the company receives. Many industry experts and telecommunications companies describe below-market pricing.[90] Thus, the Committee sought more information about Huawei's financing, including its customer financing. Such financial information would also help provide greater understanding about the financial structuring of a firm that remains largely opaque.

During the Committee's hearing, Mr. Ding suggested he did not understand and had no knowledge of the term "national champion," which is often used to describe favored Chinese companies throughout the economic literature on China.[91] The Committee finds that Mr. Ding's suggestion that he does not understand the term is not credible. Huawei itself provided Capitol Hill offices a slide presentation in November 2011, which used the term "national champion" several times.[92] In response to the Committee's questions about use of the term in that document, Huawei did not deny that it used the document and provided the document containing the term.[93] Rather, Huawei stated that the particular slide in the larger document was created by a third party and thus not Huawei's responsibility.[94] The Committee finds that Huawei's knowing use of the document in its discussions with United States elected representatives is sufficient evidence to prove that Huawei does in fact have an understanding of the term. Mr.

Ding's consistent refusal to answer questions about which firms are considered national champions in the Chinese telecommunications sector was obstructionist. In fact, his response to the Committee's question that "Huawei has not paid attention to the meaning of 'national champion' before," is obviously untrue given the company's use of the term in its presentations previously.[95] Moreover, his answers suggest that he did not want to explain how it was that Huawei, the number one telecommunications provider in China, is not a company of strategic importance in China, as recognized by others around the world.

Huawei officials also deny that they have received any special financial incentives or support from the Chinese government.[96] Huawei claimed that the company simply takes advantage of general Chinese banking opportunities, but does not seek to influence or coordinate with banks such as the Chinese Development Bank and the Export-Import Bank, which are both state owned. In previous presentations, Huawei had suggested that it served as an "intermediary and bridge" between the state-backed financial institutions and Huawei customers.[97] Huawei refused, however, to provide more detail about precisely how those lines of credit developed. Huawei also refused to answer specifics about its formal relationships with the Chinese banks, opting to simply answer that it maintains "normal business relations" with the Export-Import Bank of China.[98]

In its presentation to the Committee during the February meeting, Huawei provided a list of the Memoranda of Understanding (MOUs) it claims to have signed with Chinese banks for lines of credit for its customers.[99] Huawei admits that its customers have a US $100 billion in credit available, yet Huawei asserts that only $5.867 billion has been drawn in the period between 2005 and 2011. Further, in its written responses, Huawei states that it is a "financing opportunity available to customers, not to Huawei."[100] Yet Huawei explained at the February 23, 2012, meeting with Committee investigators that the goal of the large available credit lines was for China "to appear impressive" and that "Huawei had to participate or would no longer receive loans" from Chinese banks.[101] In response to repeated questions and document requests, Huawei failed to provide further written explanation of the benefits Huawei gains from these financing arrangements, and it did not provide internal documents or any auditable information that would substantiate its claims about the scope and processes of this financing.

Similarly, Huawei refused to describe the details of its relationships with Chinese state-owned banks. For example, in Mr. Ding's statement for the record, he explained that Huawei receives loans from ten Chinese banks. But Mr. Ding refused to answer how many of those ten banking institutions in China are state-owned.[102] As described in the previous section, Huawei also refused to provide "additional details as to [its] consultancy relationships" because it would "include highly sensitive proprietary information" governed by non-disclosure agreements.[103] In response to Committee questions about Huawei's success and whether it was owing to the company's support from the Chinese government, Huawei represented to the Committee that its relationships with and advice received from these companies are the source of the company's global success.[104] Because Huawei refuses to provide details on those relationships and advice rendered, the Committee cannot evaluate its claim that any of its success is due to these relationships. Accordingly, the Committee discounts the role played by these consulting companies, and continues to find it likely that Huawei has substantially benefited from the support of the Chinese government.

In sum, Huawei admits that its customers receive billions of dollars in support from Chinese state-owned banks and that it has received favorable loans from Chinese banks for years. Huawei refuses to provide answers to direct questions about how this support was secured, nor does it provide internal documentation or auditable financial records to evaluate its claims that the terms of these agreements comply with standard practice and international trade agreements. The Committee is equally concerned with statements by company leaders that undermine the Committee's confidence in the financial information the company has provided. For example, in a June 2007 speech to Huawei employees in the United Kingdom, Mr. Ren stated that he appreciated the subsidiary's attempt to create financial statements, "whether the data is accurate or not."[105] Based on available information, the Committee finds that Huawei receives substantial support from the Chinese government and Chinese state-owned banks, which is at least partially responsible for its position in the global marketplace.

> **viii.   Huawei failed to provide sufficient details or supporting documentation on its operations, financing, and management in the United States; evidence undermines its claims of being a completely independent subsidiary of Huawei's parent company in Shenzhen, China.**

To understand the United States' current vulnerability to supply-chain threats posed by Huawei equipment, it is necessary to know the extent to which Huawei's equipment is already placed in U.S. infrastructure. Because the U.S. telecommunications infrastructure is largely built and owned by the private sector, the U.S. government does not have the full picture of what is contained within it and thus is not yet fully informed to develop policies to protect that critical infrastructure from vulnerabilities.[106]

29

The Committee thus asked Huawei for information on its contracts for products and services within the United States. Understanding the extent to which Huawei equipment already exists in the United States is necessary to evaluate the present risk to the country, as well as to confirm Huawei's statements about the size and scope of its operations in the United States. Unfortunately, Huawei failed to provide specific information about its dealings within the United States. Huawei did provide the Committee a list of Huawei's major customers in the United States: Cricket Communications; Clearwire; Cox TMI Wireless, Hibernia Atlantic, Level 3/BTW Equipment, Suddenlink; Comcast and Bend Broadband. Huawei, however, did not provide information on the size and scope of its operations, which elements of the infrastructure it is providing, and where these operations are located.[107]

The information requested by the Committee about Huawei's contracts in the United States is also necessary to evaluate Huawei's claims that they comply with all laws and trade obligations regarding the price of their products and services.[108] To date, Huawei has failed to provide any information to validate its claims that the prices of Huawei's products are based on market conditions. Huawei's refusal to answer clearly or provide documents supporting its claims necessitates the Committee finding that Huawei's defense is not credible. The Committee considers it possible that Huawei receives substantial support from the Chinese government such that Huawei can market at least some of its products in the United States below the costs of production.

Similarly, the extent to which Huawei's subsidiaries in the United States operate independently of the parent company in Shenzhen remains unclear. Such information is important, because any connections between the parent company in China to the Chinese government might affect the operations and behavior of the company in the United States. The Committee therefore requested information on the extent to which Huawei USA's decisions are controlled, influenced, or reviewed by the parent company.

Huawei explained that the first US-based Huawei subsidiary was established in the United States in 2005 with headquarters in Plano, Texas. Huawei stated that the parent company does not require approval for individual contracts in the United States.[109] Rather, it stated that the Board of Directors in China does set general terms for operations in the United States, and the parent company can help mobilize resources and set strategy should the subsidiary need it. The Committee has heard from several former Huawei employees in the United States who dispute Huawei's explanation of its business model. Sources from around the United States have provided numerous specific instances of business decisions in the United States requiring approval by the parent company in China. In one instance, an individual with first-hand knowledge explained that senior level executives in the United States could not sign a contract for cyber-security services in the United States without approval in China. In fact, in one instance, a contract previously signed by a U.S.-based senior official at Huawei was repudiated by the parent company.[110] These employees provided documentary evidence, including internal memoranda and emails, discussing corporate policy from China. This description of Huawei's US subsidiaries also comports with reports about the ties between other Huawei subsidiaries and the parent company in China.[111]

To resolve this conflict, the Committee sought more information through its written questions to understand the precise mechanisms through which the Huawei parent company in Shenzhen controls Huawei's strategy for entry and growth into the United States market. Concerns that Beijing's support to Huawei could impact the U.S. market were heightened by Huawei officials' statements to Committee staff that Huawei USA is given general guidance and "resources" from the parent company if needed.[112] In its written response, however, Huawei failed to answer the Committee's detailed questions or provide any further information about the level of coordination between Huawei USA and the parent company.[113]

The information and material provided by Huawei employees with first-hand access coupled with Huawei's failure to provide detailed, internal information, undermines Huawei's claims. For these reasons, the Committee does not find credible Huawei's claims that its U.S. subsidiaries operate independently of the Huawei headquarters in Shenzhen, China.

ix. **Evidence shows that Huawei exhibits a pattern of disregard for the intellectual property rights of other entities and companies in the United States.**

Huawei's ability to protect intellectual property rights is an important indicator of the company's ability to abide by the laws of the United States. Thus, the Committee sought greater information on Huawei's history of IP protection.

The Committee has reason to believe that Huawei is careless with its compliance with intellectual property protections. Investigators heard from numerous sources that Huawei has a checkered history when it comes to protecting the intellectual property of other entities.[114] Specifically, several former employees of Huawei said it is known to purposely use the patented material of other firms. First-hand accounts of former employees suggest that Huawei does not appropriately purchase software applications for use by its employees.[115] Similarly, the Committee heard from industry experts that

31

Huawei has purposely used and marketed patented products of other companies.[116] Finally, the Committee is in receipt of a Huawei slide presentation that was provided to Capitol Hill offices that itself violates copyright obligations by knowingly using proprietary material from an outside, nonaffiliated consulting firm.[117]

Huawei officials consistently denied ever infringing other companies' intellectual property rights. Even with respect to the litigation with Cisco, in which Huawei agreed to remove certain products from the marketplace, Huawei asserts that it had not violated Cisco's interests.[118] Rather, Huawei suggested that the expert's review in that case of their equipment found no infringement of Cisco patents.[119]

Huawei's defense is not credible. First, with respect to the Cisco litigation, Huawei's statements do not comport with statements made by Huawei officials at the time of the lawsuit acknowledging that the company will remove infringing equipment.[120] Second, the Cisco settlement itself required Huawei to "update and change all of the products that have been accused of violating copyright or intellectual property rights."[121] Finally, during the hearing on September 13, 2012, Charles Ding refused to answer the clear question of whether Cisco code had ever been in Huawei equipment.[122] Mr. Ding's obstructionism during the hearing undermines Huawei's claims that it did not violate Cisco's patented material.

The Committee finds that Huawei's denials of intellectual property infringement were not credible or supported by available evidence. Because Huawei failed to produce any internal documents or support for its defenses, the Committee finds that Huawei has exhibited a pattern of, at the very least, reckless disregard for the intellectual property rights of other entities.

x. **Huawei failed to provide details of its operations in Iran, though it denied doing business with the government of Iran, and did not provide evidence to support its claims that it complies with all international sanctions or U.S. export laws.**

Huawei's ability to comply with international sanctions regimes and U.S. export control regulations is an important indicator of the company's ability to comply with international standards of corporate behavior and to abide by U.S. laws irrespective of China's influence or interests. Public reporting raises questions about the company's compliance with these laws.

In response to the Committee's questions, Huawei officials provided only vague assertions about their commitment to all laws. Specifically, Huawei asserted that the company seeks to abide by all legal obligations and has transformed its business practices with the help of outside consultants to better monitor its actions to ensure compliance with international sanctions regimes. To highlight the lack of influence of the Chinese regime over its decisions, Huawei indicated the Chinese Embassy in Iran was surprised by Huawei's decision to limit its business dealings in Iran. Huawei also stated that it does not allow its employees to participate in cyber activities, such as population monitoring, anywhere in Iran.

Huawei has refused, however, to answer detailed questions about its operations in Iran or other sanctioned countries. In its written submission to the Committee, Huawei again reiterated that it limited its future business in Iran because of the enhanced sanctions and an inability to collect payment for operations in Iran. Huawei highlights, though, that "Huawei respects the contracts signed with [its] customers" and thus will not end current contracts in Iran.[123] Huawei claims to "observe laws and regulations of the UN, the U.S., the E.U. and other countries and regions on sanctions."[124] It also claims to have instituted an internal program on trade compliance representing best practices to manage these issues.[125] But Huawei refused to provide any internal documents relating to its decision to scale-back operations in Iran or otherwise ensure compliance with U.S. laws.

Such documents would have validated Huawei's claims that the decision was based on legal compliance requirements and not influenced by any pressure by the Chinese government.

xi. Huawei refused to provide details on its R&D programs, and other documents undermine its claim that Huawei provides no R&D for the Chinese military or intelligence services.

To understand the extent to which Huawei performs R&D activity on behalf of the Chinese military or intelligence services, the Committee asked for information about its activities on behalf of the Chinese government or military. Specifically, the Committee requested information on the technologies, equipment, or capabilities that the funding or grants by the Chinese government was supporting. In its written submission to the Committee, Huawei failed to provide responsive answers to the Committee's questions about the specifics of government-backed R&D activities.[126] Rather, Huawei simply asserted that it only bid on R&D projects open to the rest of the industry.[127]

Huawei similarly claimed in its meetings with the Committee that it does not provide special services to the Chinese military or state security services.[128]

In its answers to the Committee's questions after the hearing, Huawei again simply asserted that it "has never managed any of the PLA's networks" and "has never been financed by the Chinese government for R&D projects for military systems." Huawei did admit, however, that it develops "transport network products, data products, videoconferencing products, and all centers, and voice over IP (VoIP) products" for the Chinese military "accounting for .1% of Huawei's total sales."[129] Huawei also claimed, however, that it "develops, researches, and manufactures communications equipment for civilian purposes only."[130]

The Committee also received internal Huawei documentation from former Huawei employees showing that Huawei provides special network services to an entity the employee believes to be an elite cyber-warfare unit within the PLA.[131] The documents appear authentic and official Huawei material, and the former employee stated that he received the material as a Huawei employee.[132] These documents suggest once again that Huawei officials may not have been forthcoming when describing the company's R&D or other activities on behalf of the PLA.

The Committee finds that Huawei's statements about its sales to the Chinese military are inherently contradictory. The Committee also finds that Huawei's failure to respond fully to questions about the details of its R&D activities, coupled with its admission that it provides products for the Chinese military and documents received from employees, undermine the credibility of its assertion that it does not perform R&D activities for the Chinese government or military.

xii. Former and current Huawei employees provided evidence of a pattern and practice of potentially illegal behavior by Huawei officials.

During the course of the investigation, several former and current Huawei employees came forward to provide statements and allegations about Huawei's activities in the United States. Given the sensitivities involved, and to protect these witnesses from retaliation or dismissal, the Committee has decided to keep the identities of these individuals confidential. The Committee has received multiple, credible reports from these individuals of several potential violations by Huawei officials. Those allegations include:

- Immigration violations;
- Bribery and corruption;
- Discriminatory behavior; and
- Copyright infringement.

Specifically, the Committee heard from numerous employees that Huawei employees visiting from China on tourist or conference visas are actually working full-time at Huawei facilities, in violation of U.S. immigration law. Similarly, Huawei employees provided credible evidence that individuals coming to the United States on particular visas, for example, for jobs requiring engineering expertise were not in fact employed by Huawei as engineers. These and other alleged violations of immigration law will be referred to the Department of Homeland Security for review and potential investigation.

Second, employees have alleged instances fraud and bribery when seeking contracts in the United States.[133] Those allegations will be referred to the Justice Department for further review and potential investigation.

Third, employees with whom the Committee spoke discussed allegations of widespread discriminatory behavior by Huawei officials. These individuals assert that it is it very difficult if not impossible for any non-Chinese national to be promoted in Huawei offices in the United States. Further, these employees assert that non-Chinese nationals are often laid-off only to be replaced by individuals on short-term visas from China.[134] These allegations will be referred to the appropriate agencies in the Executive Branch to review and consider.

Finally, the Committee heard from former Huawei employees that may constitute a pattern and practice of Huawei using pirated software in its United States facilities. As previously described, the Committee received information with Huawei's logo that knowingly and admittedly violated another firm's copyrighted material.[135] The Committee thus finds that Huawei has exhibited a careless disregard for the copyrighted material of other entities. As there may indeed be credibility to these employee allegations, the Committee will also refer these claims to the Justice Department for investigation.

B. ZTE failed to answer key questions or provide supporting documentation supporting its assertions, arguing that answering the Committee's

requests about its internal corporate activities would leave the company criminally liable under China's states-secrets laws.

ZTE sought to appear cooperative and timely with its submissions to the Committee throughout the investigation. ZTE consistently refused, however, to provide specific answers to specific questions, nor did the company provide internal documentation that would substantiate its many claims. As with Huawei, the Committee focused its review of ZTE on the company's ties to the Chinese state, as well as the company's history, management, financing, R&D, and corporate structure. The Committee did not to receive detailed answers on a number of topics described below. ZTE did not describe its formal interactions with the Chinese government. It did not provide financial information beyond that which is publicly available. It did not discuss the formal role of the ZTE Communist Party Committee and only recently provided any information on the individuals on the Committee. The Committee did not receive details on ZTE's operations and activities in Iran and other sanctioned countries. Finally, ZTE refused to provide detailed information on its operations and activities in the United States.

Importantly as well, ZTE argued at great length that it could not provide internal documentation or many answers to Committee questions given fear that the company would be in violation of China's state-secrets laws and thus subject ZTE officials to criminal prosecution in China.[136] In fact, ZTE refused even to provide the slides shown to the Committee staff during the meeting in April, 2012, for fear that they might be covered by state secrets. To the extent ZTE cannot provide detailed and supported answers to the Committee because China's laws treat such information important to the security of the Chinese regime, the Committee's core concern that ZTE's presence in the U.S. infrastructure represents a national-security concern is enhanced.

The Committee notes that ZTE's many written submissions were never numbered to align with the Committee's specific questions and document requests, as would be typical with formal legal processes. The Committee believes that, through this method, ZTE sought to avoid being candid and obvious about which questions it refused to answer. Moreover, ZTE's answers were often repetitive, lacking in documentary or other evidentiary support, or otherwise incomplete.

The Committee also notes that ZTE did not simply deny all national-security concerns arising from the global telecommunications supply chain. ZTE has advocated for a solution – one based on a trusted delivery model – in which approved "independent third-party assessors" transfer "hardware, software, firmware, and other structural elements in the equipment to the assessor."[137] Such a model, as advocated by ZTE, would include among other things, a "thorough review and analysis of software codes," "vulnerability scans and penetration test," "review of hardware design and audit of schematic system diagram," "physical facility review and independent comprehensive audit of vendor's manufacturing, warehousing, processing, and delivery operations," "periodic assessments."

ZTE suggests that a model, as previously proposed by Huawei and other companies, and similar in some respects to that introduced in United Kingdom, be implemented across the spectrum for telecommunications equipment providers. As discussed above, the Committee remains concerned that, although mitigation measures can be of some assistance, this model fails to appreciate the nature of telecommunications equipment.

i. ZTE did not alleviate Committee concerns about the control of Chinese state-owned enterprises in ZTE's business decisions and operations.

As with Huawei, the Committee is concerned with the influence of the Chinese state in ZTE's operations. Such access or influence would provide a ready means for the Chinese government to exploit the telecommunications infrastructure containing ZTE equipment for its own purposes. To evaluate the ties to the Chinese state, the Committee focused on the company's history, structure, and management. Many commentators have noted that ZTE's founding included significant investment and involvement by Chinese state-owned enterprises, and thus the Committee sought to unpack the current operations and ownership structure with the hope of understanding whether there are remaining ties to the Chinese state.

ZTE describes itself as a global provider of telecommunications equipment and network solutions across 140 countries. Founded in 1985, ZTE states that its 2011 revenue led the industry with a 24% increase to $13.7 billion; its overseas operating revenue grew 30% to U.S. $7.42 billion during the period, accounting for 54.2% of overall operating revenue.[138] ZTE markets itself by explaining that its systems and equipment have been used by top operators in markets around the world. Importantly, ZTE also highlighted in its 2011 Annual Report that China's 12th five-year national plan has significantly contributed to ZTE's recent domestic success.[139]

During the interviews with ZTE officials in April and May 2012, ZTE officials stressed that ZTE is a publicly traded company, having been listed on the Shenzhen stock exchange in 1997, and the Hong Kong stock exchange in 2004. ZTE contends that it did not begin with government assistance, either with technology transfers or financial assistance. Rather, ZTE stated that the Chinese government became a shareholder during the 1997 public offering. ZTE has also asserted that the state-owned-enterprise shareholders have no influence on strategic direction of the company.[140] ZTE officials often contrasted themselves with Huawei, though often did not mention Huawei by name. In particular, officials suggested that Huawei is ZTE's main competitor, but often stated that ZTE is more transparent since it is a publicly traded company.

These officials often relied on this public listing to claim that ZTE finances are transparent and comply with both Chinese and Hong Kong regulations regarding financial disclosures. The officials often simply referred to the fact that they have annual reports that detail information requested, such as amount and extent of government loans, subsidies, and credits. ZTE refused, however, to explain whether it would be willing to meet the reporting and transparency requirements of a western stock exchange such as the New York Stock Exchange.[141] As with Huawei, when the Committee sought more detailed answers from ZTE on its interactions with key government agencies, ZTE refused to answer.

The history and structure of ZTE, as admitted by the company in its submissions to the Committee, reveal a company that has current and historical ties to the Chinese government and key military research institutes. In response to questioning, the ZTE officials first discounted and seemingly contradicted their own public statements, which suggest that ZTE formed originally from the Ministry of Aerospace, a government agency. In fact, exhibits displayed during the meeting in Shenzhen highlighted an early collaboration between ZTE and the government-run No. 691 Factory, and other state-owned enterprises. ZTE refused to provide the Committee copies of the slides presented during this meeting.

ZTE officials instead suggested that Mr. Hou Weigui founded ZTE in 1985 with five other "pioneer" engineers. Although they had all previously worked for state owned enterprises, ZTE officials insisted that the formation of ZTE did not arise from any relationship with the government. The company's written submission to the Committee admits that the company had an early connection to No. 691 Factory, which was established by the Chinese government.[142] As described by ZTE, No. 691 Factory is now known as Xi'an Microelectronics Company, and is a subsidiary of China Aerospace Electronics Technology Research Institute, a state-owned research institute. In its submission, ZTE admits that Xi'an Microelectronics owns 34% of Zhongxingxin, a shareholder of ZTE.[143] ZTE's evolution from research entities with connections to the Chinese government and military highlight the nature of the information-technology (IT) sector in China. In fact, taking as true ZTE's submission of its history and ownership,

ZTE's evolution confirms the suspicions of analysts who study the IT sector in China and describe it as a hybrid serving both commercial and military needs.[144]

In 1997, ZTE was publicly listed for the first time on the Shenzhen stock exchange. ZTE executives claim that it was at this point that other state owned enterprises began investing in ZTE.

Currently, 30% of ZTE is owned by Zhongxinxin group and the remaining 70% is held by dispersed public shareholders. The Committee is particularly interested in whether the 30% ownership by Zhongxingxin constitutes a controlling interest or otherwise provides the state owned enterprises an opportunity to exert influence over the company. This question is particularly relevant because two state owned enterprises own 51% of Zhongxingxin. ZTE executives stressed that the public ownership of ZTE is increasing as Zhongxingxin sells its shares (for example, in 2004, Zhongxingxin owned 44% of ZTE, and now Zhongxingxin holds only 30%). In ZTE's July 3 submission to the Committee, ZTE states that "[v]ery few knowledgeable individuals in China would characterize ZTE as a state-owned entity (SOE) or a government-controlled company."[145] But the Committee specifically asked how it is that ZTE remains accountable to its shareholders and not influenced or controlled by its largest shareholder given this ownership structure. In its submission to the Committee, ZTE admits that a 30% share is the point at which Hong Kong and Chinese law considers the holder to be a "controlling shareholder."[146] ZTE simply stated that the company's fiduciary duty to the numerous shareholders means that the controlling shareholder does not in fact exert much actual control over the company.[147] ZTE does not explain in more detail how the Board members, five of whom are chosen by state-owned enterprises, and some of whom are acknowledged members of the Chinese Communist Party and members of ZTE's internal Communist Party Committee, would not exert any influence over the decisions of the company.

Zhongxingxin, ZTE's largest shareholder is owned in part by two state-owned enterprises, Xi'an Microelectronics and Aerospace Guangyu, both of which not only have ownership ties to the Chinese government, but also allegedly partake in sensitive technological research and development for the Chinese government and military. ZTE failed to address the Committee's questions seeking detailed information on the history and mission of these two companies. ZTE also failed to answer questions about these companies' relationship to key leaders within ZTE, specifically Mr. Weigu Hou, and ZTE's other major shareholder, Zhongzing WXT.

Because ZTE failed to answer key questions about its history and the connections to government institutions, the Committee cannot trust that it is free of state influence, particularly through its major shareholders and Board members.

ii. **ZTE maintains a Chinese Party Committee within the company, and has not fully clarified how that Committee functions, who chooses its members, and what relationship it has with the larger Chinese Communist Party.**

As with Huawei, ZTE's connection to the Chinese Communist Party is a key concern for the Committee. Such a connection offers the Party the opportunity to influence the decisions and operations of a company seeking to expand into the critical infrastructure in the United States. As described previously, the modern Chinese state-capitalistic economy is largely influenced if not controlled by the Party, in large part through the party committees that exist within individual firms.

During interviews with ZTE officials, ZTE refused to answer whether the executives or board members are members of the Chinese Communist Party. ZTE first downplayed the existence of the Party Committee within ZTE, and company representatives were unable to answer whether any members of the Board were also members of the state Party. Subsequently, in response to continued Committee questions, ZTE acknowledged that it does, in fact, contain an internal Committee Party, which ZTE suggests is required by the laws of China.[148] In response to the Committee's written questions, ZTE again refused, however, to provide information about the names and duties of the Party Committee members. At the September 13, 2012, hearing, Mr. Zhu attested under oath that ZTE would provide the names of those individuals on the Party Committee.[149]

In response to questions posed at the September 13, 2012, hearing ZTE did provide the Committee a list of 19 individuals who serve on the Communist Party Committee within ZTE. At least two of those individuals appear to be on the ZTE Board of Directors. Other individuals are major shareholders in ZTE entities. ZTE has requested and the Committee has agreed to keep the names of these individuals out of the public domain. ZTE discounts the influence of that these individuals may have over the company. The company asked that the Committee not release the names of the individuals for fear that the company or the individuals might face retaliation by the Chinese government or Communist Party. The Committee has decided to keep the names of those members out of this public report, but the company's concern with the potential retaliatory measures it faces by the government for simply providing the

Committee the names of an internal ZTE body highlights why this Committee remains very concerned that the Chinese state is, or could be, responsible for the actions of the company. China clearly seeks to maintain deep ties into and secrecy about its role in economic actors in China. The control Chinese government maintains over the company's actions and level of transparency is of particular concern when that company seeks to build critical U.S. infrastructure.

ZTE also did not fully explain the function of the Party Committee. Instead, ZTE simply states that the Party Committee is controlled by company management. This assertion is contradicted by ZTE's own statement that ZTE executives and board members actually are members of the [Chinese Communist Party] and delimit its activities."[150] To the extent these executives and Board Members have obligations to both the company's shareholders and the State through the Communist Party, there is an inherent conflict of interest in their duties, and this statement provides confirmation that the Party likely does in fact have influence and input into the business affairs of the company through these individuals.

The affidavit by the independent director, Timothy Steinert, seeks to allay any concerns of influence by the government or Party by stating that:

> In my experience and to my knowledge, no member of ZTE's Board of Directors has raised for consideration an interest on behalf of the Chinese Government, the People's Liberation Army or the Chinese Communist Party.[151]

This statement does not resolve the Committee's concerns. First, there is a range of operational and strategic decisions made on a daily basis within companies that are not decided by or reviewed by the Board. Mr. Steinert's affidavit says nothing about the role of the Party Committee in those decisions prior to their reaching the Board, or for decisions that do not reach the Board at all. Second, the Party's influence through ZTE's Party Committee may not be facially obvious in the decision documents appearing for review to the Board. Since at least two members of the Board are also members of the Chinese State Party, it is impossible to know whether the votes of the Board are conducted without influence by the Chinese Communist Party. When considering ZTE's activities or voting on certain measures, those Board members need not cite the Party to be acting on the state's behalf or in pursuit of the state's interests. For these reasons, the Committee finds unpersuasive ZTE's claims that Mr. Steinert's affidavit "confirms that ZTE business decision making is not influence by the government or Party considerations"[152]

ZTE recently suggested that the Party Committee "performs only ceremonial and social functions." For six months, the Committee has asked ZTE about the role of the Party Committee, but only at the final hour, did it provide any response at all. Without further information and specifics about the role and influence of the Party Committee in the operations of the company, the Committee simply cannot allay the concerns about the internal party apparatus existing within a company seeking to build U.S. critical infrastructure.

iii.   ZTE failed to disclose information about its activities in the United States.

ZTE discussed its extensive presence in 140 countries, but significantly downplayed any potential threats to the U.S., by suggesting that 95% of its U.S. sales are from handsets. ZTE officials highlighted that they have five R&D centers in the U.S. employing about 300 people. ZTE officials attempted to suggest that the company's presence in rural infrastructure and networks was to assist the U.S. effort with its rural broadband plans. Committee staff questioned this logic, and ZTE officials admitted that ZTE's role in these projects were not for charity or public service, as they had initially suggested, but to get a "foothold" in the country and learn the technology in the United States. ZTE officials even admitted that they are willing to provide this equipment to the U.S. below cost in order to learn the U.S. market. Specifically, during the Committee's meeting with ZTE officials in Shenzhen, Mr. Zhu stated that the company was willing to lose money on projects in the United States to get a foothold in the United States and to understand the technology and standards in the United States.

ZTE's description of its current U.S. activity is simply a picture at a particular point in time. The Committee could not confirm the extent of the company's contracts or access to the United States market absent responses to the Committee's document requests.[153] Despite numerous requests, ZTE has not provided detailed information on infrastructure projects in the United States.[154] ZTE also failed to answer follow-up questions that would explain whether ZTE purposely bids on projects below cost and how the company is able to sustain these losses. Further, at the HPSCI hearing on September 13, Mr. Zhu reversed his previous answers and refused to acknowledge that ZTE ever bids below cost for projects in the United States.[155]

iv.   ZTE failed to provide any answers or evidence about its compliance with intellectual property or U.S. export-control laws.

The protection of intellectual property and compliance with United States export control laws are a core concern for U.S. interests. The ability of a company to comply with these laws provide a useful test of that company's ability to follow international codes of business conduct and remain free of undue state influence.

Representatives of the company consistently declined to comment on recent media reports that ZTE had sold export-controlled items to Iran.[156] At the hearing on September 13, 2012, ZTE acknowledged that it is performing an internal review to determine if the company destroyed any documents or other evidence related to its activities in Iran.[157] Mr. Zhu provided no information that could allow the Committee to evaluate the extent of those activities, their compliance with U.S. laws, or management's involvement in the potential destruction of documents and evidence. ZTE did not answer in specific written questions from the Committee asking why it sought to limit its Iranian business activities; whether ZTE will honor its current contracts in Iran; or whether those contracts include training or maintenance of surveillance equipment. Further, ZTE refused to answer questions about what products ZTE resold in Iran. ZTE also refused to provide any documents on its activities in Iran.

v.   **ZTE failed to provide clear answers to Committee questions about its R&D activities, particularly as they relate to any military or government projects.**

Given ZTE's background, the Committee was interested in ZTE's R&D activities, and particularly its R&D activities with or on behalf of the Chinese military or security services. This information would help the Committee evaluate whether a company seeking to build critical infrastructure in the United States could also be working with the Chinese government on R&D projects with the purpose of finding or exploiting vulnerabilities in those systems.

ZTE's known connections to Chinese government-related research institutes are of particular interest. For example, ZTE acknowledges that one of its primary shareholders, Zhongxingxin, is owned in part by Xi'an Microelectronics, a subsidiary of China Aerospace Electronics Technology Research Institute, a state-owned research institute.[158] Another 17% of Zhongxingxin is held by Aerospace Guangyu, a subsidiary of a state-owned enterprise whose business includes production of, among other things, aerospace technology products.[159] ZTE failed to answer questions from the Committee seeking further details about the range of products theses research institute have produced on the Chinese government so the committee could not evaluate whether those technologies were produced for military or intelligence purposes.[160]

These ties to Chinese government research institutes and production companies, the Committee sought more information on the details of ZTE's R&D activities, and particularly its potential work on behalf of the government, military, or security services. ZTE was proud to explain that it had established 18 state-of-the-art R&D centers throughout China, France, and India, and to employ over 30,000 research professionals. ZTE further claims that 10% of the company's annual revenue is invested in R&D. ZTE failed, however, to answer Committee questions about the technologies it may create or sell to the Chinese government and military. During the Committee's April 12, 2012 meeting with company officials, Mr. Steinert, the independent board member, stated that, ZTE's work on behalf of the Chinese telecommunications providers that happen to be state-owned enterprises does not suggest that ZTE does work on behalf of the military or intelligence services. When providing written answers ZTE refused to provide clear answers about the nature and extent of any work it does on behalf of the Chinese military or security services. Rather, ZTE states that "[t]he funding ZTE has received from government or consortia during the past several years is indistinguishable from similar funding available throughout the world in companies engaged in R&D through normal procurement processes."[161]

To the extent ZTE's R&D activities are simply in response to standard government procurement processes, the Committee does not understand why it refuses to answer direct questions about the details of those projects. For this reason, the Committee cannot allay concerns that ZTE is aligned with Chinese military and intelligence activities or research institutes.

Conclusion and Recommendations

The Committee launched this investigation to seek answers to some persistent questions about the Chinese telecommunications companies Huawei and ZTE and their ties to the Chinese government. Throughout the months-long investigation, both Huawei and ZTE sought to describe, in different terms, why neither company is a threat to U.S. national-security interests. Unfortunately, neither ZTE nor Huawei have cooperated fully with the investigation, and both companies have failed to provide documents or other evidence that would substantiate their claims or lend support for their narratives.

Huawei, in particular, provided evasive, nonresponsive, or incomplete answers to questions at the heart of the security issues posed. The failure of these companies to provide responsive answers about their relationships with and support by the Chinese government provides further doubt as to their ability to abide by international rules.

Recommendations

Based on this investigation, the Committee provides the following recommendations:

Recommendation 1: The United States should view with suspicion the continued penetration of the U.S. telecommunications market by Chinese telecommunications companies.

- The United States Intelligence Community (IC) must remain vigilant and focused on this threat. The IC should actively seek to keep cleared private sector actors as informed of the threat as possible.

- The Committee on Foreign Investment in the United States (CFIUS) must block acquisitions, takeovers, or mergers involving Huawei and ZTE given the threat to U.S. national security interests. Legislative proposals seeking to expand CFIUS to include purchasing agreements should receive thorough consideration by relevant Congressional committees.

- U.S. government systems, particularly sensitive systems, should not include Huawei or ZTE equipment, including in component parts. Similarly, government contractors – particularly those working on contracts for sensitive U.S. programs – should exclude ZTE or Huawei equipment in their systems.

Recommendation 2: Private-sector entities in the United States are strongly encouraged to consider the long-term security risks associated with doing business with either ZTE or Huawei for equipment or services. U.S. network providers and systems developers are strongly encouraged to seek other vendors for their projects. Based on available classified and unclassified information, Huawei and ZTE cannot be trusted to be free of foreign state influence and thus pose a security threat to the United States and to our systems.

Recommendation 3: Committees of jurisdiction within the U.S. Congress and enforcement agencies within the Executive Branch should investigate the unfair trade practices of the Chinese telecommunications sector, paying particular attention to China's continued financial support for key companies.

Recommendation 4: Chinese companies should quickly become more open and transparent, including listing on western stock exchange with advanced transparency requirements, offering more consistent review by independent third-party evaluators of their financial information and cyber-security processes, complying with U.S. legal standards of information and evidentiary production, and obeying all intellectual-property laws and standards. Huawei, in particular, must become more transparent and responsive to U.S. legal obligations.

Recommendation 5: Committees of jurisdiction in the U.S. Congress should consider potential legislation to better address the risk posed by telecommunications companies with nation-state ties or otherwise not clearly trusted to build critical infrastructure. Such legislation could include increasing information sharing among private sector entities, and an expanded role for the CFIUS process to include purchasing agreements.

---

[1] Ken Hu, "Huawei Open Letter." http://online.wsj.com/public/resources/documents/Huawei20110205.pdf (accessed August 2, 2012).

[2] Huawei's letter was issued in February, 2011, when the Committee on Foreign Investment in the United States (CFIUS) issued a recommendation that Huawei voluntarily divest assets it received in a 2010 deal with 3Leaf, a United States company that developed advanced computer technologies. Shayndi Raice, "Panel Poised to Recommend Against Huawei Deal," *Wall Street Journal*, February, 11, 2011. http://www.wsj.com/article/SB20001424052748704629004576136340771329706 html (accessed August 2, 2012)

[3] A classified annex to this report provides both classified information relevant to the discussion, as well as information about the resources and priorities of the IC.

[4] Steven M. Rinaldi, James P. Peerenboom, and Terrence K. Kelly, "Identifying, Understanding, and Analyzing Critical Infrastructure Interdependencies," *IEEE Control Systems Magazine*, December 2001.

[5] "The former National Counterintelligence Executive, Mr. Robert Bryant, recently noted that, 'Insider threats remain the top counterintelligence challenge to our community.' An insider threat arises when a person with authorized access to U.S. Government resources, to include personnel, facilities, information, equipment, networks, and systems, uses that access to harm the security of the United States. Malicious insiders can inflict incalculable damage. They enable the enemy to plant boots behind our lines and can compromise our nation's most important endeavors. Over the past century, the most damaging U.S. counterintelligence failures were perpetrated by a trusted insider with ulterior motives." http://www ncix.gov/issues/ithreat/index.php

[6] FBI, *Intelligence Bulletin*, "Supply Chain Poisoning: A Threat to the Integrity of Trusted Software and Hardware," June 27, 2011: 1.

[7] Office of National Counterintelligence Executive, *Report to Congress on Foreign Economic Collection and Industrial Espionage*, "Foreign Spies Stealing US Economic Secrets in Cyberspace."(October 2011, Washington, DC: 1.)

[8] United States Congress, *2011 Annual Report of U.S.-China Economic and Security Review*. (2011, Washington DC: 59.)

[9] National Institute of Standards and Technology, *Draft NISTIR 7622*, "Piloting Supply Chain Risk Management for Federal Information Systems," June 2010, 28.

[10] Joint Press Conference, March, 29, 2012, Sydney, Australia. http://www.pm.gov.au/press-office/transcript-joint-press-conference-sydney-1.

[11] The Economist, "Huawei: The Company that Spooked the World," *Economist*, August, 4, 2012. http://www.economist.com/node/21559929 (accessed September 30, 2012).

[12] United States Congress, *2011 Annual Report of U.S.-China Economic and Security Review*. (2011, Washington DC: 148.)

[13] Office of National Counterintelligence Executive, *Report to Congress on Foreign Economic Collection and Industrial Espionage*, "Foreign Spies Stealing US Economic Secrets in Cyberspace."(October 2011, Washington, DC: i.)

[14] Ibid, 5; HPSCI staff interviews with cyber-security experts.

[15] Ibid, 5.

[16] Defense Science Board, *Report on Mission Impact of Foreign Influence on DoD Software*, September 2007: viii.

[17] "Where State security requires, a State security organ may inspect the electronic communication instruments and appliances and other similar equipment and installations belonging to any organization or individual." State-Security Law of the People's Republic of China, Article 11.

[18] Defense Science Board, *Report on Mission Impact of Foreign Influence on DoD Software*, September 2007: viii.

[19] Northrop Grumman Corp, *Occupying the Information High Ground: Chinese Capabilities for Computer Network Operations and Cyber Espionage*, prepared for U.S.-China Economic and Security Review Commission, March 7, 2012, 6-8.

[20] The Economist, "The Long March of the Invisible Mr. Ren," *the Economist*, June 2, 2011. http://www.economist.com/node/18771640 (accessed on September 15, 2012).

[21] FBI, *Intelligence Bulletin*, "Supply Chain Poisoning: A Threat to the Integrity of Trusted Software and Hardware," June 27, 2011: 4.

[22] ZTE, *Submissions to HPSCI*, July 3, 2012; ZTE, *Submission to HPSCI*, August 3, 2012; Ken Hu, "Huawei Open Letter." http://online.wsj.com/public/resources/documents/Huawei20110205.pdf (accessed August 2, 2012). John Suffolk, Huawei's Global Security Officer, previously served as the Chief Information Officer with the UK government at a time when the UK entered into its agreement with Huawei to set up the Cyber Security Evaluation Center (CSEC). Mr. Suffolk advocated for a cyber-security and supply-chain solution that would recognizing the issues as a global concern that must be addressed at an international level, preferably by an international standards-setting organization through which all products must pass. Mr. Suffolk also highlighted that in the present age, technology is moving faster than our ability to adapt our institutions. Key assumptions are that security requires a whole systems approach, and that all systems will be breached at some point. Thus, in Mr. Suffolk's view, telecommunications companies and governments must manage the risk, focus on areas of most concern, instill diversity and adaptability, and learn to deal with the consequences. Mr. Suffolk acknowledged that Huawei's desire to be an end-to-end provider for whole network solutions does not align with his proposed solutions to the supply-chain concerns, which depend on diversity of supply. HPSCI meeting with John Suffolk, February 23, 2012.

[23] Anderson, R., & Fuloria, S. Certification *and Evaluation: A Security Economics Perspective. Emerging Technologies and Factory Automation*, (2009).

[24] Ken Thompson, *Reflections on Trusting Trust. Turing Award Lecture*, (1984).

[25] Gerwin Klein, Formal Verification of an OS Kernel. *Symposium on Operating Systems Principles*. Big Sky, MT, USA: Association of Computing Machinery, (2009).

[26] Daniel Jackson, Martyn Thomas, and Lynette I. Millett, Eds. *Software for Dependable Systems: Sufficient Evidence? Committee on Certifiably Dependable Software Systems*, National Research Council. (National Academies Press, 2007.)

[27] Rules of the House of Representatives, 112th Congress, Rules 10(3)(m), 11.

[28] Understanding and developing a strategy to protect the country from Chinese cyber espionage in the United States is one of the obligations of U.S. counterintelligence professionals. Many reports have suggested that the Intelligence Community continues to struggle integrating and acting on its counterintelligence mission. As Michelle Van Cleave, former head of the National Counterintelligence Executive, has explained, "the U.S. government has been slow to appreciate the effects of foreign intelligence operations, much less to address the threats they pose to current U.S. foreign policy objectives or enduring national security interests." Michelle Van Cleave, "Chapter 2: The NCIX and the National Counterintelligence Mission: What Has Worked, What Has Not, and Why," in *Meeting Twenty-First Century Security Challenges*, 62.

Office of National Counterintelligence Executive, *Report to Congress on Foreign Economic Collection and Industrial Espionage*, "Foreign Spies Stealing US Economic Secrets in Cyberspace."(October 2011, Washington, DC)

[30] In response to the Committee's June 12, 2012, document request, ZTE provided one document: a summary of its cyber-security measures. Huawei provided no documents other than materials already on the company's website or otherwise publicly released. After the September 13, 2012 hearing, Huawei provided a document labeled "Internal Compliance Program (ICP)," dated March 2012. That document summarizes Huawei's internal policy with respect to trade control policies. Huawei provided no material that would allow the Committee to evaluate their compliance with or enforcement of that policy. Huawei also provided a copy of the publicly released paper entitled "Cyber Security Perspectives" prepared by John Suffolk, and Huawei's public statement regarding its Commercial Operations in Iran.

[31] House Permanent Select Committee on Intelligence, *Hearing on Investigation of the Security Threat Posed by Chinese Telecommunications Companies Huawei and ZTE,* 112th Congress, 2nd session (September 13, 2012).

[32] Given the sensitivities involved, and to protect these witnesses from retaliation or dismissal, the Committee decided to keep the identities of these individuals confidential.

[33] As the U.S.-China Commission has highlighted, even the largely circumstantial evidence that known incidents appear state sponsored is compelling -- as the actors' targeting often focuses on key defense and foreign-policy sources of information, which are of most concern to the state and not commercial entities. United States Congress, *2011 Annual Report of U.S.-China Economic and Security Review.* (2011, Washington DC: 59.)

[35] United States Congress, *2011 Annual Report of U.S.-China Economic and Security Review.* (2011, Washington DC: 59-60.)

[36] ZTE, *Submission to HPSCI*, July 3, 2012, 3.

[37] Discussion with PLA Piper, June 2012. Huawei, in its responses to Questions for the Record after the September 13, 2012, hearing, denied that there is any state-secret concern with their documentation. The Committee is left wondering, then, why Huawei has refused to provide internal documentation that could substantiate its claims. Moreover, Huawei's failure to provide the list of individuals on Huawei's Chinese Communist Party Committee is an example in which the Committee believes the state's concerns with state secrets is particularly relevant. Huawei's continuous failure to provide such information cannot be explained otherwise.

[38] Huawei Investment & Holding Co., Ltd., *2011 Annual Report*, 7.

[39] Ken Hu, "Huawei Open Letter." http://online.wsj.com/public/resources/documents/Huawei20110205.pdf (accessed August 2, 2012).

[40] That report suggests that Huawei "was founded in 1988 by Ren Zhengfei, a former director of the PLA General Staff Department's Information Engineering Academy, which is responsible for telecom research for the Chinese military. Huawei maintains deep ties with the Chinese military, which serves a multi-faceted role as an important customer, as well as Huawei's political patron and research and development partner. Both the government and the military tout Huawei as a national champion, and the company is currently China's largest, fastest-growing, and most impressive telecommunications-equipment manufacturer. Evan Medeiros et al., *A New Direction for China's Defense Industry*, Rand Corporation: 218-219. http://www.rand.org/pubs/monographs/2005/RAND_MG334.pdf.

[41] Ibid, 217-219

[42] The Economist, "Huawei: The Company that Spooked the World," *Economist*, August, 4, 2012. http://www.economist.com/node/21559929 (accessed September 30, 2012).

[43] Juha Saarinen, "Analysis: Who Really Owns Huawei?," *ITNews*, May 28, 2012.

[44] Ken Hu, "Huawei Open Letter." http://online.wsj.com/public/resources/documents/Huawei20110205.pdf (accessed August 2, 2012).

[45] Richard McGregor, *The Party: The Secret World of China's Communist Rulers*, 2010: 204.

[46] Huawei, *Submission to HPSCI*, July 3, 2012.

[47] House Permanent Select Committee on Intelligence, *Hearing on Investigation of the Security Threat Posed by Chinese Telecommunications Companies Huawei and ZTE,* 112th Congress, 2nd session (September 13, 2012).

[48] Huawei Investment & Holding Co., Ltd., *2011 Annual Report,* 2.

[49] Huawei, *September 25, 2012 Response to Questions for the Record,* at __.

[50] Huawei, *September 25, 2012 Responses to Questions for the Record,* 6-7.

[51] Interviews with Huawei officials, February 23, 2012.

[52] Interviews with Huawei officials, February 23, 2012.

[53] Interviews with Huawei officials, February 23, 2012.

[54] Mike Rogers and Dutch Ruppersburg, letter to Huawei, June 12, 2012; Huawei, *letter to HPSCI,* "Response to June 12, 2012 Letter," July 3, 2012.

[55] Huawei, *Documents Provided in Advance of February 23, 2012 entitled Shareholder Agreements.*

[56] John Lee, "The Other Side of Huawei," *Business Spectator,* March 30, 2012.

[57] United States Congress, *2011 Annual Report of U.S.-China Economic and Security Review.* (2011, Washington DC: 59)

[58] Ibid.

[59] House Permanent Select Committee on Intelligence, *Hearing on Investigation of the Security Threat Posed by Chinese Telecommunications Companies Huawei and ZTE,* 112th Congress, 2nd session (September 13, 2012).

[60] Huawei, *Submission to House Permanent Select Committee on Intelligence,* July 3, 2012, 1.

[61] Ibid.

[62] Ibid.

[63] Huawei, *July 2, 2012 Submission,* 7-15

[64] Highlighting that as China moved from a pure control economy in the 1990s, Chinese companies experienced particular difficulties raising capital in foreign capital markets, including the "most sensitive of all, how would they explain the role of the internal party bodies, which for years had run companies, free of any of the inconvenient structuring of corporate reporting and governance rules." Richard McGregor, *The Party: The Secret World of China's Communist Rulers,* 2010: 47; *See* John Lee, "The Other Side of Huawei," *Business Spectator,* March 30, 2012

[65] Huawei, *Submission to House Permanent Select Committee on Intelligence,* July 3, 2012, 2.

[66] Ibid.

[67] *See* John Lee, "The Other Side of Huawei," *Business Spectator,* March 30, 2012; Richard McGregor, *The Party: The Secret World of China's Communist Rulers,* 2010.

[68] Richard McGregor, *The Party: The Secret World of China's Communist Rulers,* 2010: 72.

[69] Meeting with Mr. Ren, May 23, 2012.

[70] Huawei, *Submission to House Permanent Select Committee on Intelligence,* July 3, 2012.

[71] Huawei officials stated that China had cancelled ranking system at the time. HPSCI Interviews with Huawei officials, February 23, 2012.

[72] Huawei officials suggested that the rumors that Mr. Ren is a former PLA General is the result of confusion with Julong, another Chinese telecommunications company and state-owned enterprise whose President is a Major General in the PLA. HPSCI Interviews with Huawei officials, February 13, 2012.

[73] Huawei, *September 25, 2012 Responses to HPSCI Questions for the Record,* 8.

[74] Huawei, *September 25, 2012 Responses to HPSCI Questions for the Record,* 8.

[75] Huawei asserted that Chen Jinyang, who invested 3,500 RMB, was a 26-year-old manager at the Chinese Trade Department.

[76] Interviews with Huawei officials, February 23, 2012.

[77] Interviews with Huawei officials, February 23, 2012.

[78] Interview with Ken Hu, February 23, 2012.

[79] Scholars of the Chinese political economy suggest that national champions are those chosen by China to be supported both financially and otherwise by the state because of the strategic importance of the sector and the company to China's national interests. *See* John Lee, "The Other Side of Huawei," *Business Spectator,* March 30, 2012

[80] Huawei, *Submission to House Permanent Select Committee on Intelligence*, July 3, 2012, 19.

[81] Ibid.

[82] Interviews with Huawei officials, February 23, 2012; Huawei presentation, February 23, 2012.

[83] Interviews with Huawei officials, February 23, 2012

[84] Huawei, *Submission to House Permanent Select Committee on Intelligence*, July 3, 2012, 19-20.

[85] Mike Rogers and Dutch Ruppersburg, letter to Huawei, June 12, 2012, 6.

[86] Huawei, *Submission to House Permanent Select Committee on Intelligence*, July 3, 2012, 19-20.

[87] Phone conversations with Huawei representatives, June 2012.

[88] Huawei, *Submission to House Permanent Select Committee on Intelligence*, July 3, 2012, 20-21.

[89] John Lee, "The Other Side of Huawei," *Business Spectator*, March 30, 2012.

[90] The Economist, Huawei: The Company that Spooked the World," *Economist*, August, 4, 2012. http://www.economist.com/node/21559929 (accessed September 30, 2012);

[91] House Permanent Select Committee on Intelligence, *Hearing on Investigation of the Security Threat Posed by Chinese Telecommunications Companies Huawei and ZTE,* 112th Congress, 2nd session (September 13, 2012).

[92] Huawei, *Slide Presentation dated November 2011*, 8.

[93] Huawei, *Responses to HPSCI Questions for the Record*, September 25, 2012, 1.

[94] Ibid.

[95] Ibid.

[96] Inteviews with Huawei officials, February 23, 2012

[97] Huawei, *Corporate Presentation*, February 23, 2012, 26.

[98] Huawei, *Submission to House Permanent Select Committee on Intelligence*, July 3, 2012, 2.

[99] Huawei, *Corporate Presentation*, February 23, 2012, 27.

[100] Huawei, *Responses to HPSCI Questions for the Record*, September 25, 2012, 2.

[101] Inteviews with Huawei officials, February 23, 2012.

[102] House Permanent Select Committee on Intelligence, *Hearing on Investigation of the Security Threat Posed by Chinese Telecommunications Companies Huawei and ZTE,* 112th Congress, 2nd session (September 13, 2012).

[103] Huawei, *Submission to House Permanent Select Committee on Intelligence*, July 3, 2012, 21.

[104] Interviews with Huawei officials, February 23, 2012.

[105] Ren Zhengfei, speech at Huawei BT Division & Huawei UK, June 30, 2007, quoted in Huawei magazine *Improvement*, Issue 58.

[106] The Commerce Department, working with the Defense Department, has sought information from the private sector to better understand the entire scope of cyber-risks facing the country's critical telecommunication infrastructure. The Commerce issued a survey under the Defense Production Act to dozens of U.S. based companies to gather better information on the security of their networks. The review of that information is still ongoing.

[107] The Committee has offered on numerous occasions to provide Huawei an opportunity to provide the information the Committee needs to evaluate the security of U.S. networks in a closed forum or under an agreement to provide such information confidentially. Huawei has continuously refused to accept any such offer, option instead to simply assert that such details are confidential. The Committee intends to continue evaluating these issues and plans to approach Huawei in the future for more details on these contracts to fulfill the Committee's duty to evaluate the risk posed by these firms.

[108] House Committee on Foreign Affairs, *Hearing on Unfair Trade Practices against the US*, 112th Congress, 2nd session (July 19, 2012).

[109] Interview with Huawei officials, February 23, 2012.

[110] Interview with Employees.

[111] John Lee, "The Other Side of Huawei," *Business Spectator*, March 30, 2012.

[112] Interview with Huawei officials, February 23, 2012.

[113] Huawei, *Submission to House Permanent Select Committee on Intelligence*, July 3, 2012.

[114] Interview with Huawei Employees.

[115] Interview with Huawei Employees.

[116] Interview with industry experts.

[117] Huawei representatives admitted to Committee staff that using this presentation was in violation of McKinsey's copyright protections, and that McKinsey and Huawei have no business relationship thus undermining any claim that Huawei had a right to use the slide. Huawei, *Slide Presentation dated November 2011*, 8 (using McKinsey & Co. material).

[118] Interview with Huawei Officials, February 13, 2012.

[119] Ibid.

[120] Marguerite Reardon, "Huawei Admits Copying," *Light Reading*, March 25, 2003. http://www.lightreading.com/document.asp?doc_id=30269 (accessed on August 13, 2012)

[121] Ibid.

[122] House Permanent Select Committee on Intelligence, *Hearing on Investigation of the Security Threat Posed by Chinese Telecommunications Companies Huawei and ZTE*, 112th Congress, 2nd session (September 13, 2012).

[123] Huawei, *Submission to House Permanent Select Committee on Intelligence*, July 3, 2012, 6.

[124] Ibid.

[125] Ibid, 5-6.

[126] Ibid, 3-4.

[127] Ibid, 3.

[128] Interviews with Huawei officials, February 23, 2012.

[129] Huawei, *September 25, 2012 Responses to Questions for the Record*, 12.

[130] Ibid.

[131] Internal Huawei email, dated July 1, 2011.

[132] Ibid.

[133] Interviews with former Huawei employees.

[134] Interviews with former Huawei employees.

[135] Huawei, *Slide Presentation dated November 2011*, 8.

[136] ZTE August 3, 2012 submission, at 12-17.

[137] ZTE, *Submissions to HPSCI*, August 3, 2012, 23.

[138] ZTE, *2011 Annual Report*, 68-69.

[139] "The national '12th Five Year Plan' has provided driving force for the further development of the domestic telecommunications industry." ZTE, *2011 Annual Report*, 69.

[140] Meeting with ZTE officials, April 12, 2012, Shenzhen, China.

[141] ZTE, *Submissions to HPSCI*, July 3, 2012.

[142] Ibid, 4.

[143] Ibid.

[144] As a report commissioned by the U.S. China-Commission stated: "The IT sector in China can be considered a hybrid defense industry, able to operate with success in commercial markets while meeting the demands of its military customers. The Chinese telecommunications market is heavily influenced by its largest domestic members—such as hardware and networking giants Huawei Shenzhen Technology Company, Zhongxing Telecom (ZTE), and Datang Telecom Technology Co., Limited. These companies and some smaller players are not always directly linked to the PLA or C4ISR modernization because of their strong domestic and international commercial orientation. The digital triangle model, however, allows them to benefit directly from a background network of state research institutes and government funding in programs that do have affiliation or sponsorship of the PLA." Northrop Grumman Corp, *Occupying the Information High Ground: Chinese Capabilities for Computer Network Operations and Cyber Espionage*, prepared for U.S.-China Economic and Security Review Commission, March 7, 2012, 69.

[145] ZTE, *Submissions to HPSCI*, July 3, 2012, 2.

[146] Ibid, 9

[147] Ibid.

[148] Ibid, 4.

[149] House Permanent Select Committee on Intelligence,*Hearing on Investigation of the Security Threat Posed by Chinese Telecommunications Companies Huawei and ZTE,* 112th Congress, 2nd session (September 13, 2012).

[150] John Merrigan, letter to Katie Wheelbarger, September 28, 2012.

[151] Affidavit of Timothy Steinert, at para. 6.

[152] ZTE, *Submissions to HPSCI,* August 3, 2012, 5.

[153] Meeting with ZTE officials, April 12, 2012, Shenzen, China.

[154] Ibid.

[155] House Permanent Select Committee on Intelligence, *Hearing on Investigation of the Security Threat Posed by Chinese Telecommunications Companies Huawei and ZTE,* 112th Congress, 2nd session (September 13, 2012).

[156] Ellen Nakashima,"Chinese telecom firm ZTE probed for alleged sale of U.S. surveillance equipment to Iran," *Washington Post,* July 13, 2012. http://www.washingtonpost.com/world/national-security/chinese-telecom-firm-zte-probed-for-alleged-sale-of-us-surveillance-equipment-to-iran/2012/07/13/gJQA6mKUiW_story.html.

[157] House Permanent Select Committee on Intelligence, *Hearing on Investigation of the Security Threat Posed by Chinese Telecommunications Companies Huawei and ZTE,* 112th Congress, 2nd session (September 13, 2012).

[158] ZTE, *Submissions to HPSCI,* April 2012, 4.

[159] Ibid.

[160] Ibid.

[161] ZTE, *Submissions to HPSCI,* July 3, 2012, 17.

www.ingramcontent.com/pod-product-compliance
Lightning Source LLC
Chambersburg PA
CBHW080540290526

45790CB00006B/2488